RAISED TO BE A SOLDIER

Understanding and Removing the Armor We Wear from Childhood Trauma

RAISED TO BE A SOLDIER

*Understanding and Removing the
Armor We Wear from Childhood Trauma*

KELLY A. NENEZIAN, LMHC

ethos
collective

Raised to Be a Soldier © 2025 by Kelly A. Nenezian. All rights reserved.

Printed in the United States of America

Published by Igniting Souls
PO Box 43, Powell, OH 43065
IgnitingSouls.com

This book contains material protected under international and federal copyright laws and treaties. Any unauthorized reprint or use of this material is prohibited. No part of this book may be reproduced or transmitted in any form or by any means, electronic or mechanical, including photocopying, recording, or by any information storage and retrieval system, without express written permission from the author.

LCCN: 2025902910
Paperback ISBN: 978-1-63680-469-9
Hardcover ISBN: 978-1-63680-470-5
e-book ISBN: 978-1-63680-471-2

Available in paperback, hardcover, e-book, and audiobook.

Any Internet addresses (websites, blogs, etc.) and telephone numbers printed in this book are offered as a resource. They are not intended in any way to be or imply an endorsement by Igniting Souls, nor does Igniting Souls vouch for the content of these sites and numbers for the life of this book.

The information provided in this book is intended for general informational purposes only and should not be construed as mental health or medical advice. The content is based on the author's personal experiences and research and is not a substitute for professional medical care, diagnosis, or treatment. Always consult with a qualified healthcare provider before making any changes to your diet, exercise routine, or mental health practices.

This book discusses trauma, gives examples of traumatic situations, and gives some case examples of clients with trauma, which may trigger your trauma. It is strongly recommended that you are under the care of a licensed mental health professional to process anything brought up while reading this book. If you are experiencing a medical condition, mental health issues, or any symptoms that require medical attention, please seek the guidance of a licensed healthcare professional. If you are in crisis, call the National Crisis Hotline at 988 or visit your local emergency room. The author and publisher are not responsible for any adverse effects or consequences resulting from the use of the information provided in this book.

Some names and identifying details may have been changed to protect the privacy of individuals.

This book is dedicated to my mom,
Theresa P. Nenezian.
To the moon and back, Mom.

TABLE OF CONTENTS

Foreword by Elias H. Sarkis, MD ix
Introduction xiii
Chapter 1: Our First Battleground 1
Chapter 2: Armor Selection through Adaptation 13
Chapter 3: The Different Armor We Wear 31
Chapter 4: Elusive Armor 56
Chapter 5: Need Armor. 67
Chapter 6: Endurance Armor 79
Chapter 7: Control Armor. 92
Chapter 8: Perfection Armor 106
Chapter 9: Factors That Keep Us Enlisted. 116
Chapter 10: Ceasefire 138
Chapter 11: Allies in Healing 157
Endnotes. 161
Acknowledgments. 167
About the Author 171

FOREWORD

BY ELIAS H. SARKIS, MD

I am honored to write the foreword to this clear, insightful, and compassionate guide to somatic psychotherapy. This book will be invaluable to clients and clinicians alike.

Ms. Nenezian's writing style is accessible to the general public, yet comprehensive and deeply informed. She skillfully explains the childhood origins of trauma and how early experiences—whether overt or subtle—can shape the way we respond to life in adulthood. Through vivid and relatable case examples, she illustrates how these patterns emerge, many of which resonate with stories I've heard from my patients.

The author draws on a growing body of research to demonstrate that adverse childhood experiences affect mental health as well as physical well-being. She weaves together recent discoveries and foundational studies, offering readers a wide-ranging yet cohesive understanding of trauma. Her exploration of the biological underpinnings is especially compelling, covering areas such as epigenetics, brain circuitry, and the intergenerational transmission of trauma. She also considers how trauma may begin even before birth, influenced by prenatal experiences and environmental stressors.

Ms. Nenezian places all of this within the context of how individuals adapt to meet familial and societal expectations—what it means to be "successful" in a world that often demands we hide our pain. She illuminates how these pressures shape our identities and how the strategies we adopt to survive in childhood transform into obstacles in adulthood.

One of the most powerful metaphors in the book is that of the armored soldier. Just as a soldier dons protective gear to survive the battlefield, we develop emotional armor to survive the challenges of early life. While this armor may serve us as children, it can become limiting or possibly harmful in adulthood. The author gently guides readers toward understanding how this armor forms—and how it can be safely and gradually shed.

She draws inspiration from the pioneering work of Alexander Lowen, particularly his theory of character structure, and integrates it with insights from the Enneagram to create a holistic framework for understanding the mind-body connection. Her synthesis is original and deeply respectful of their traditions.

Importantly, the author destigmatizes mental illness by highlighting its developmental roots. She shows that our emotional struggles are not personal failings but adaptations to earlier wounds. Her compassionate approach can help reduce the shame many feel for not living up to societal or familial ideals—and that, in itself, may be the first step in someone's healing journey.

She also offers a clear-eyed critique of the limitations of the biomedical model, which often favors diagnosis and medication over deeper exploration. While acknowledging that medications can be helpful—and at times necessary—for symptom relief, she reminds us that medication alone does not constitute true healing. The true work of healing is only done by in-depth psychotherapy. A wealth of research supports what many therapists already know: the combination of medication and psychotherapy is far more effective than either approach alone.

Perhaps my favorite part of the book is her candid and grounded description of her therapeutic work. She shows us how she meets clients where they are, often tuning into her own bodily responses to better understand what her clients might be holding unconsciously. Her use of Bioenergetic Analysis, rooted in Alexander Lowen's work, is brought to life through concrete, real-world examples. Her comparison of somatic patterns to the Enneagram types adds another layer of insight, enriching clinical understanding and personal reflection.

Most importantly, this book offers hope. Ms. Nenezian traces a therapeutic path forward—a way for clients to reconnect with their bodies, release what no longer serves them, and live fuller, more integrated lives. In her hands, somatic psychotherapy becomes more than a treatment; it becomes a journey of transformation.

—Elias H. Sarkis, MD

INTRODUCTION

As a licensed therapist, I have helped many individuals, raised as "soldiers," to remove the armor they donned after experiencing childhood trauma. My training in deep-level healing and somatic interventions permits the body to recover and the patient to reintegrate mind, body, and soul. My work is to help individuals understand their true selves, accept themselves as they are, and learn to interact in the world in a way that feels authentic and safe for them.

In the first few chapters of this book, I describe how I've come to conceptualize the complex nature of mental health diagnoses within our Western model, how we engage with these diagnoses, and how they intersect with trauma. It's impossible to talk about trauma without addressing other diagnoses, as they are deeply interconnected in complex ways. Our Westernized model makes it difficult to truly understand mental health, as it primarily caters to insurance companies and systems, not people. I strive to articulate this intricate perspective, though I don't claim to have all the answers. My language may not be perfect, and it will likely evolve as we continue to learn and develop more nuanced models of understanding.

Throughout this book, I have included several common armoring patterns exhibited in individuals with childhood trauma. These armoring patterns are rooted in Dr. Alexander Lowen's character structures, which are used in his somatic therapy modality, Bioenergetic Analysis. Bioenergetic Therapy integrates the body and mind. I view the armoring patterns similarly to Lowen's character structures, but also differently.

Lowen developed Bioenergetic Analysis in the 1950s. This body-oriented psychotherapy emphasizes the connection between emotional well-being and physical vitality. The therapy operates under the premise that the body stores trauma, repressed emotions, and unexpressed psychological conflicts, which can manifest as chronic muscle tension, posture distortions, and energy blockages. Through a combination of physical exercises, breathing techniques, and verbal expression, Bioenergetic Therapy aims to release these physical tensions and promote a healthier flow of energy, leading to emotional release and greater psychological integration.

Bioenergetic Therapy targets character structures, what I label armoring patterns, that individuals develop in response to early emotional pain. By focusing on bodily sensations and encouraging clients to engage with their physical experiences, Bioenergetic Therapy breaks down the barriers to emotional expression and fosters self-awareness. The therapeutic process often includes exercises designed to bring attention to breathing, grounding, and bodily sensations, enabling individuals to access and process deep-seated emotional material.

The body-oriented nature of Bioenergetic Therapy has generated interest among researchers seeking to explore the mind-body connection in therapeutic contexts. Many studies have demonstrated that bioenergetic exercises significantly reduced symptoms of anxiety and depression in participants. A study by Bourguignon explored the efficacy of Bioenergetic Analysis, a body-oriented psychotherapy, in treating mental health conditions such as depression and anxiety.[1] The research found that combining Bioenergetic Therapy with traditional talk therapy led to significant improvements in emotional regulation, as well as a reduction in somatic symptoms related to depression. Participants reported feeling more grounded and relaxed, highlighting the therapeutic potential

Introduction

of Bioenergetic techniques in addressing both psychological and physical aspects of mental health. The study underscores the importance of integrating body-focused therapies into mental health treatment plans for holistic healing.

The available evidence supports Bioenergetic Therapy as an effective tool for addressing somatic complaints, chronic tension, and emotional trauma. One key strength of Bioenergetic Therapy is its holistic approach, which integrates bodywork into the healing process. This integration provides an alternative pathway for individuals who may struggle with more traditional verbal therapies. It is important to note that Bioenergetic Therapy may not be suitable for all clients, particularly those who have significant physical limitations or difficulties engaging in physical exercises. Due to the intense nature of Bioenergetic Analysis, I always recommend that a client complete some talk therapy before participating in it.

It is important to know that we can have all the armoring patterns discussed in the following chapters, which are common. Typically, we have a dominant pattern at the beginning of treatment. These armoring patterns create physical, psychological, relational, and energetic patterns that therapists can observe for diagnosis and treatment. It is also important to note that, as with every aspect of mental health, each armoring pattern has a spectrum of intensity. Exposure to more chronic and more intense trauma patterns tends to yield more intense representations of the armoring patterns or thicker armor.

There are also a wide variety of ways we can experience the developmental or childhood trauma that most often causes these wounding patterns. I cannot discuss all of them in this book. However, the underlying shame messages and armoring patterns may help identify armoring patterns, even if the story doesn't quite fit. A trained Bioenergetic therapist can help identify an armoring pattern even if it isn't easily defined by the client's perception of their story.

I also included Enneagrams that may be associated with the defensive pattern described in the chapter. The Enneagram has become popular in recent years, and it can offer a bridge to the armoring patterns discussed in this book. I believe Enneagrams have excellent insights into a soldier's armoring and offer a unique perspective many find helpful.

I discuss healing in each chapter and at the end of the book. Many extremely helpful somatic modalities for treating trauma are available, some of which I will highlight in the final chapter. Due to my work and knowledge acquired through practice and research studies, literature, and mentors, I believe that healing trauma should include both physical and psychological components to be genuinely beneficial and promote long-term, sustainable change.

Please note that any exercises or techniques should be done with a psychotherapist trained in the treatment modalities chosen. Our bodies are designed to need an external regulator in moments of emotion, and therefore, deep healing work should be done with the support of a trusted professional who can guide you in and out of the exercises. This book is in no way encouraging the use of these techniques. Not every exercise is for every person, and a trained professional can help you determine which exercises may be helpful.

A special note to any parents reading this book: This book may be difficult for you to read as you raise children or if you have raised children. While doing your own childhood trauma work, such as reading this book, you may realize that you, unintentionally, may have continued your childhood trauma patterns in some way with your child. It may also be unpleasant to recognize that you may have participated in some of the patterns mentioned in this book before you were aware of them. Please, be gentle with yourself. Your healing is worthwhile, and healing for others is possible through your healing. Stick with it.

CHAPTER 1

OUR FIRST BATTLEGROUND

It is a grave injustice to a child or adult to insist that they stop crying. One can comfort a person who is crying which enables him to relax and makes further crying unnecessary; but to humiliate a crying child is to increase his pain, and augment his rigidity. We stop other people from crying because we cannot stand the sounds and movements of their bodies. It threatens our own rigidity. It induces similar feelings in ourselves which we dare not express and it evokes a resonance in our own bodies which we resist.

—Dr. Alexander Lowen

Imagine you are twelve years old, it's five o'clock, and your dad gets home in thirty minutes. The type of day he has had and whether he stops for a drink on the way home will dictate whether or not the night ends in abuse. The dread in your stomach grows as the clock hands inch closer to five thirty, and he still hasn't come home, which means he will come home drunk.

He's much more likely to lose his temper when he's drunk. Mom doesn't stand up for you when he gets like that, and you can't understand why. Maybe it's because you aren't worth standing up for, you think to yourself. He never hits you, the different objects he throws miss you every time, so it isn't abuse, right? Sometimes, he gets mad. That's all.

Then you wonder how you can protect yourself. He got mad yesterday when you said hello to him; don't do that again. Two weeks ago, he threw dishes at you because they weren't done; make sure to wash the dishes. Quickly! He ripped up the painting you made in art class; don't show him this time.

Your brain races along with your heart. You can't cry; you have too much to do. Both mom and dad get mad when you cry anyway. You hold your breath as the door opens at a quarter after seven. You go to your room, hoping he won't care to find you tonight. If anyone is going to keep you safe, it's you.

Each time Dad gets mad, you learn what not to do, and you won't do it anymore. You dream of the day you will have learned everything there is to learn, and he won't get mad at you anymore. You just need to be better. You can do this. So, hold your breath, pay attention, and be a soldier.

Boot Camp

From the earliest moments of life, children are immersed in a rich tapestry of emotions. Joy dances in their laughter, curiosity sparkles in their eyes, and love flows freely in their tender embraces. Life is full of the vibrant reality of freedom. Freedom to feel, to move, to sing, to be.

Yet, alongside these bright hues, darker shades lurk in the shadows, waiting to be acknowledged and understood. A child shouts with joy, but a parent's angry tone tells them to be quiet. Children cry when they can't have their way to grieve what they cannot understand, and a parent tells them they are being a brat and need to be quiet. Children are taught at a very young age to stop feeling and start pretending. They undergo training in an emotional boot camp where repression, suppression, and dissociation become the battle strategies that they will carry through life. These little soldiers learn to be tough, hide their emotions, and fight through whatever battles lie ahead.

As children navigate the complexities of their emotions, they often encounter barriers that hinder their ability to express themselves. Societal expectations, familial dynamics, and personal insecurities create layers of protection around the heart, shielding it from the raw intensity of feeling. Fear, shame, and guilt weave a delicate veil, obscuring an emotion's actual depth, leaving it cloaked in ambiguity and mystery.

For many children, the journey of emotional repression begins in the tender embrace of infancy. From the moment they enter the world, they are bombarded with messages about what is acceptable and what is not. Tears are suppressed, anger is silenced, and vulnerability is considered weakness. In this environment, emotions become tangled in a web of confusion, their true essence distorted by the weight of societal expectations.

As children grow older, the pressure to conform intensifies, and the mask of repression grows ever thicker. They learn to hide their true feelings behind a façade of indifference, fearing the consequences of vulnerability. Forced smiles replace tears, a veneer of politeness suppresses anger, and guarded gestures rather than open affection express love.

From a young age, we learn to obey others above ourselves. For example, even if we don't want to, our parents tell us to say hello. If we don't, they say, "Oh, she is being silly or shy." Right away, we learn to make others comfortable even if we feel uncomfortable. They are teaching us to ignore our body's natural and adaptive mechanisms that make us feel safe.

We have an overwhelming and biological need for love and connection. So, our thinking brain is always trying to figure out how to get it, even if that is at the expense of ourselves, especially to get love and connection from our parents or primary caregivers. We are taught how we "should" act to receive love and attention, which leads to generations of holding emotions within our bodies. It leads to emotional and physical disease. It leads to a war within ourselves. It leads to fighting through life. It leads to creating traumatized soldiers.

Childhood is like a boot camp. We are supposed to learn how to interact with life during the developmental stages of childhood. We learn how to enjoy life when things are going well and how to navigate life when it goes wrong. We learn how to live and how to be alive. Our brain undergoes rapid changes in our first few years of life. We begin to learn how to move around and talk, and we are supposed to learn how to process and express our emotions. However, my experience is that boot camp often doesn't involve healthy lessons on emotional expression for many of us. It either involves emotional neglect, which doesn't teach us how to navigate our emotional health, leading to patterns of emotional dysregulation, or emotional chaos or abuse, which involves us trying to keep those around us steady enough so we can feel safe. In these cases, we learn to repress our emotions. We graduate from boot camp hypervigilant and reactive, or emotionally numb and restricted, or both.

There has been a misconception that trauma symptoms only present for individuals who have experienced physical abuse, sexual abuse, and a singular atrocious event. Individuals who go through overwhelming events, such as those mentioned, are absolutely likely to experience trauma symptoms. However, trauma can also come from more consistent and seemingly subtle events that cause the person experiencing them to view the world in a different way than they would have if the events hadn't occurred.

Trauma originates from a person's inability to fully emotionally process an overwhelming event with support and comfort. Studies prove that our brain becomes traumatized when we experience an emotionally triggering event, and we are unable to emotionally process the event. The strongest predictor for Post-Traumatic Stress Disorder (PTSD) and Complex Post-Traumatic Stress Disorder (CPTSD) is peri-traumatic dissociation, which defines a complex array of ways we avoid processing emotions related to a traumatic event. Simply put, post-traumatic stress symptoms are a direct result of emotional repression. Therefore, if children are taught to repress emotion through their emotional boot camp, they are much more likely to experience post-traumatic stress symptoms.

Simply put, post-traumatic stress symptoms are a direct result of emotional repression.

We must be taught how to process our emotions rather than expect to be applauded for disconnecting from them. Children raised by parents who are uncomfortable with emotional expression or adverse to it are much more likely to experience symptoms related to post-traumatic stress than those raised in emotionally connected households.

As children, we need to be taught how to process emotions, even the most intense emotions, and we are meant to be given comfort to do so, so that later on, we know that processing the most intense emotions is a safe process. This is the number one way to prevent trauma symptoms during childhood or later in life. For most of us, it is likely we will, at some point in life, experience an overwhelming event that could lead to trauma symptoms. Our caretakers can't always change what we may experience, but they can change how we experience it by teaching us how to process even the most difficult events. How we learn to process emotions in our childhood bootcamp will be how we are trained to do this in our adult life. So ask yourself, how were you taught to process emotions? Were you provided support and comfort, or shamed into hiding your emotions? How does that relate to how you process emotions now?

The Societal Battleground

You wake up to an alarm; it's another day. You contemplate snoozing for ten more minutes, but the feeling of dread rises as your to-do list runs through your mind. You feel the flutter of fear in your chest as you play in your head what you may face throughout the day. However, you've no time to think that now, or you won't be able to face the day. As you dress, your body dons its weighty armor; you tense your jaw, restrict your neck, and lock your knees. You vow to get through the day, even if you don't enjoy it. You will fight through the day; after all, you are a soldier.

The Daily War

> *The modern individual is committed to being successful, not to being a person. He belongs rightly to the action generation whose motto is do more but feel less.*
>
> —Dr. Alexander Lowen

Our world is designed to operate uniformly, yet its inhabitants are not the same. This mismatch can lead to mental health struggles as we begin to feel flawed because we can't navigate the world as easily as others. I believe the issue lies in how the world operates, not how we do. When someone's way of operating doesn't align with the world's design, daily life can feel especially challenging. Tasks that come easily to some may feel threatening to your core needs. Getting out of bed can feel overwhelming. The harder it is to function in the world, the more stress you experience, and the more overwhelmed you become, making you feel increasingly flawed. Your body recognizes the need for healing and safety, making societal demands seem less motivating and less significant. Yet, the pressure to conform doesn't lessen. Daily life stops feeling like a playground and starts feeling like a battleground. It's exhausting.

The body doesn't care about all the errands you need to run or how your life appears to others; it only cares about you. Your body is designed to keep you alive and safe. Its main focus is your well-being. This is why some individuals feel they "can't control themselves" or know what they need to do but can't make themselves do it! Much like a child will throw a tantrum and protest when their autonomy is threatened, our body will protest aspects of life that are not serving us in the moment. Even if we believe these aspects are essential, our bodies must agree. It takes a lot to logically fight against that protest for healing, which leads to many mental health struggles.

Our emotional stress response adapts to help us fight through situations. It senses an approaching bear and allows us to be hypervigilant and energetic enough to escape. However, life has become more complicated. Instead of running from bears, which most of us don't do often, we run from bills, relational stressors, and work stress. We run from our autonomy being threatened or feeling that we are losing control. Things that we can't necessarily fix with our stress response activate our nervous system. However, our body still responds in the same way with a buildup of these hormones. This hormonal buildup leads to consistent hyperarousal of our nervous system, which causes hypervigilance, low thresholds for stress, avoidance behaviors, exhaustion, reactivity, defensiveness, muscular tension, and an all-around stressful existence in our own lives.

> **Things that we can't necessarily fix with our stress response activate our nervous system.**

Those with trauma have often been taught to care more about what others think than whether they are truly happy.

We enter death alone, even if surrounded by loved ones, yet we live for everyone else.

When I refer to soldiers, I am not only talking about those who fight in foreign wars. I am referencing how we learn to live our lives, much like soldiers learn how to live through war. When referring to armor, I am not speaking of helmets and bulletproof vests, but rather the muscular tension and the defensive psychological, emotional, and energetic patterns we use to protect ourselves every day as we exist in the world around us. At one point, these patterns kept us alive and sane, but now limit our ability to really live.

I have had the pleasure of working with several soldiers in my career, and they have been a significant influence on this book. Many veterans I have had the pleasure of working with return from their service with wide eyes and tense bodies. They no longer feel much. They represent stoicism both physically and emotionally; they had to for survival. One veteran told me that the armed forces culture taught them that to survive, they must disconnect from their feelings and do whatever is necessary to keep themselves and their comrades alive. He described this as an emptying he could feel occurring in his body. He could tell when it disconnected him from his emotions and his body. He described it as if he couldn't turn his brain off. He spent every moment thinking about how he would get through the next challenge. At night, he lay awake, screening ideas for how he could do better as a soldier.

Like many of his fellow soldiers, he used alcohol to sleep. When he returned from war, he realized he had to keep fighting, but this battle was different. There was no place for him to come back into his body; he needed to keep soldiering on for his family now. They needed him to walk back into the role of husband, father, brother, and son, but he had no idea how to connect. No one he knew knew him anymore. He didn't know himself, and there was no space for him to find himself. He felt his heart beating rapidly at the sound of a car backfiring. He was physically out of the war zone, but his mind was still fighting.

This is a traditional example of a soldier. I ask you, though, to see how much of this soldier's life you relate to. Were you taught to suck it up and move forward no matter what happens and how it feels? Do you lie awake at night wondering how to face your next battle? Do you feel lost building battle strategies to fix your marriage, pay your bills, or deal with a problem at work? Do you feel you have more obligation in life than pleasure? Is your life about overcoming, or is it about being and living? You may be physically out of the war, but your mind may still be at war.

Many of us power through life. We learned our value lies in what we can do, not in who we are. We learn to work continuously to get ahead, always fight to be better, smarter, and faster. We have lost sight of the feeling of being. We no longer stand still and enjoy the air we breathe or the ground we walk upon. We no longer look into the eyes of our friends, family, and children to connect with curiosity about who they are and who we are with them. The dreams we have now are chasing money, power, and fame to achieve something, but what? Safety.

Is your life about overcoming, or is it about being and living?

Most of us are fighting daily to reach a place where we have the safety and the time just to be free and without fear. However, we never achieve this goal. Even if we achieve the false idea of safety our culture has built, if we have not processed and healed the trauma we carry, we will never feel safe. No matter how much we achieve, we can't achieve the feeling of safety through accomplishment. We die on this battlefield, hoping we leave a head start for our children. Although we were raised to be and exist as soldiers, fighting for freedom, peace, and safety within our lives, we will never truly reach those goals because we can't recognize when it is safe to stop fighting. We don't slow down long enough to realize when we are safe and our needs have been met. We never fully let ourselves enter the life we create.

This leads to some of the most intense loneliness I have ever witnessed in my client sessions because we are all fighting our own battles alone, with little time to emotionally connect with others. We live different lives while experiencing the same emotions, but we feel alienated. We scream alone in our cars and cry alone in the shower. We are truly alone. This is one of the most tragic aspects of our human existence. Expectations, repression, disconnection, and loneliness form the landscape for the battle we face and can't win.

Intergenerational Battleground

Let's say you have been in therapy for five years now. You have processed, grieved, cried, and expressed anger, but still you feel empty. You go home to be around your family, and they don't know you anymore. They don't know that you have a new understanding of them, that they may now even know themselves. You try to bridge the gap and ask your dad why he left you around the man who abused you. You wonder why he didn't protect you. You say, "Your father abused you, but you let him abuse me and turned a blind eye." Sadly, he doesn't know what you mean. He wasn't abused as severely as the other kids he grew up with. It wasn't that bad. No one protected him, so why would you need protection? The lesson: Be like your dad. Be tough. Be a soldier. Something is wrong with YOU if you let this bother you.

The battles we face often do not start with us, even if they end with us. On a larger scale, many of the wars countries fight are about multiple issues. They often encompass a present issue that is a part of generations of history. This is also true in the realm of mental health. Our battles rarely, if ever, are all our own.

Often, trauma has been normalized within families and is then continued. For instance, someone who was verbally abused during their childhood is more likely to be more desensitized to being verbally abused or seeing others be verbally abused in the future, which can lead to perpetuation of the cycle. In some cases, individuals who endured abuse can become hypersensitive instead. This can lead to other maladaptive behaviors that perpetuate other aspects of trauma if not addressed. The truth is, if we don't understand and heal our trauma, it will continue in some way, generationally.

Intergenerational trauma is a huge factor in somatic healing and finding freedom. It often involves one soldier or generations of soldiers recognizing that they no longer want to fight the war their ancestors have been fighting for generations. It consists of shifting the normalization of trauma to the recognition and exposure of trauma patterns acting as the family's battle strategies. Some of the common battle strategies within families are denying emotions and actions, normalization of bad or abusive behaviors, comparing emotions and suffering—which creates competition—minimizing emotions and experiences, and shaming natural emotional expression and natural impulses.

One of the primary reasons I encourage somatic approaches is that they have some ability to address intergenerational trauma. Intergenerational trauma refers to the transmission of trauma across multiple generations, where the effects of traumatic events or experiences experienced by one generation can affect the psychological, emotional, and physical well-being of subsequent generations. We see this type of trauma in families or communities that have faced significant historical, social, or environmental stressors, such as war, genocide, systemic oppression, abuse, or addiction. The concept of intergenerational trauma suggests that the impacts of these experiences can become embedded in familial and societal systems, affecting the descendants' behaviors, relationships, and coping mechanisms.

Take some time to see if you can identify any trauma patterns in your family system.

CHAPTER 2

ARMOR SELECTION THROUGH ADAPTATION

The primary nature of every human being is to be open to life and love. Being guarded, armoured, distrustful and enclosed is second nature in our culture. It is the means we adopt to protect ourselves against being hurt, but when such attitudes become characterological or structured in the personality, they constitute a more severe hurt and create a greater crippling than the one originally suffered.

—Dr. Alexander Lowen

In this book, I am focusing on childhood trauma and how this leads to armoring patterns that inhibit the lives of those wearing that armor. Armor selection involves many complex factors, including but not limited to the type of trauma that occurs, the age at which the trauma occurs, and genetic predispositions. Children will select their armor based on these factors in order to adapt to the trauma they face. Let's look deeper into what trauma is and how our bodies respond to it.

Trauma

Trauma refers to a deeply distressing or disturbing experience that overwhelms the brain's ability to cope, often leaving lasting emotional, psychological, or physical effects. Traumatic events can be overt and obvious, but also covert and subtle. It is important to understand that trauma is not defined by the event that occurs but rather the physiological response of our brain and body to the event(s). If the brain becomes overwhelmed and is unable to process the event, trauma symptoms occur.

Throughout my career, I have learned that the event that occurs is less important, and what truly matters is how the brain processes the event. This processing is very important; I have had individuals, such as clients, family members of clients, and people I run into outside of my work, dictate what is allowed to be traumatic and what isn't. The truth is, no one, even the individual who endured the traumatic event, decides what is traumatic; your brain does.

Childhood trauma specifically involves such experiences occurring during a person's formative years, typically before the age of 18, when the brain and sense of self are still developing. Because children lack the mature coping mechanisms of adults, trauma at this stage can profoundly shape a child's identity and sense of self, leading to extensive struggles in all areas of functioning later in life. These children often learn to shape themselves into who they believe they are *supposed* to be, rather than who they truly are. The age at which trauma occurs can define the armor that develops due to specific developmental needs at the time of the traumatic event(s). It is important to note that the ages that define the development of each armoring pattern are the most common ages, and variation from this standard is possible.

I've seen many examples of how this plays out, and I'll share a few here. For instance, if a caregiver shames children for making mistakes, those children may begin to construct an identity around perfection. If the children lose a parent and their grief makes others uncomfortable, they might suppress that grief entirely. Depending on the age they are when they lose their parent, they will develop some type of armor. Or, if a caregiver tells children they're too needy, they may develop a complicated relationship with their needs and try to deny them altogether. These are just a few ways children adapt in an effort to please those they depend on, not just out of love, but because they feel their survival is tied to being accepted and loved by their caretakers. For children, safety is simple: if their caretakers love and accept them, then they are safe. If they don't, they are in danger of not being cared for and because they cannot care for themselves, this means they are unsafe. Therefore, pleasing their caretakers becomes the main focus to ensure safety.

Due to this, they often begin to repress vital parts of their humanity—parts essential for well-being later in life—all in an effort to belong. This repression can give rise to chronic shame, a core component in the development of trauma-related disorders. Complex Post-Traumatic Stress Disorder (CPTSD) often stems from the repeated suppression of our authentic selves, particularly our true emotions, in order to fit in. And whenever we disconnect from who we truly are, emotional dysregulation and dysfunction inevitably follow.

Complex Post-Traumatic Stress Disorder is only recently being discussed as a diagnosis as we understand more clearly the complexity of mental health. CPTSD is a psychological condition that arises from prolonged or repeated exposure to trauma, often involving situations where the individual feels trapped, powerless, or unable to escape. Unlike traditional PTSD, typically linked to a single traumatic event, CPTSD is associated with ongoing or multiple traumatic experiences. Previously, people with CPTSD were diagnosed with a variety of other diagnoses, such as depression, anxiety, bipolar disorder, and many others, as therapists tried to define the array of symptoms people experience. These clients typically enter a professional office with a long list of diagnoses.

Early trauma alters brain development in regions involved in stress regulation, such as the amygdala and prefrontal cortex, leading to heightened emotional reactivity and difficulties with emotional regulation. Moreover, trauma can profoundly influence a person's worldview and coping mechanisms, often resulting in maladaptive patterns of thinking, such as catastrophizing and negative self-beliefs. These cognitive distortions contribute to the development of conditions like depression and anxiety.[2] These patterns of thinking are a direct result of how the brain was wired through neural connections during the emotional boot camp of childhood. In the case of CPTSD, it is nearly impossible to sustainably change the pattern of thinking without healing the trauma that caused the connections to form through reprocessing.

Although the events that cause the trauma response occur when a child is young, childhood trauma does not solely affect the individual during childhood. It has long-term psychological effects, often influencing an individual's behavior and emotional responses well into adulthood. This is why trauma that occurred years or even decades ago can have a lasting impact on the individual.

It does not matter how long ago the traumatic event(s) occurred; what matters is how adaptively the individual has processed the trauma. For instance, van der Kolk argues that trauma leads to dysregulation in the autonomic nervous system, which, in turn, affects emotional processing and stress responses.[3] These effects are long-term and possibly even lifelong if left untreated. As a result of the brain's change in functioning, trauma survivors may develop mental health disorders as a consequence of an immediate chemical imbalance, but also due to ongoing psychological and physiological dysregulation. This dysregulation leads to issues in relationships, inability to function at work and school, and physical health issues, which I will discuss in more detail shortly.

    Frequently, we think of our mind and bodies as separate entities: Physical disease is physical, and mental health disorders are mental. Physical illness occurs in the body, and psychological disorders arise in the mind. However, this could not be further from the truth. The mind strategizes and creates templates and maps, and it plans how we will interact with the world; the body carries out those plans. The body sends information to the mind about what it senses, giving the mind input to create its master plan of function. If there is a battle, the body is the entire platoon, fighting and taking in information that it instantly relays to the platoon's general, the mind, so that it can access battle strategies stored from former battles in real time. Much of this we do unconsciously. These two parts of us are connected; we cannot separate them, and therefore, treatment for physical and mental disorders cannot involve only one.

The Role of Mental Health Diagnosis

The pervasive and dominant narrative in mental health has historically focused on the idea that mental health diagnoses are disorders that arise from brain dysfunctions, whether caused by neurotransmitter imbalances, genetic factors, or other biological mechanisms. This "biomedical model" views conditions such as depression, anxiety, schizophrenia, and bipolar disorder as primarily rooted in physical anomalies or chemical imbalances.

    While this biological model has some truth and has led to valuable treatments (e.g., antidepressants and antipsychotics) and advanced our understanding of certain pathophysiological aspects of mental illness, it often reduces complex human experiences to a set of chemicals or brain structures.

This reductionist approach fails to account for the significant psychological, social, and environmental factors that also contribute to mental health disorders. We can compare it to knowing that 93 percent of cancers are caused by how our body interacts with our environment, such as what we eat, breathe, and other external factors, not simple genetic predisposition. We know that for nearly all diagnoses—from schizophrenia to depression—our environment is a factor.

One of the most significant psychological factors in the development of mental health disorders is trauma, particularly childhood trauma. Research from the Adverse Childhood Experiences (ACE) study has provided compelling evidence that early trauma—abuse, neglect, or household dysfunction—is strongly linked to an increased risk of mental health disorders in adulthood. Felitti demonstrated that individuals with high ACE scores were significantly more likely to develop depression, anxiety, PTSD, and substance use disorders.[4] Complex mechanisms underlying this association involve both psychological and biological factors.

We know, through research, that trauma is a factor in nearly all mental health disorders, including schizophrenia. In the case of schizophrenia, as an example, we know through research that genetics is not a primary component of the disorder; although they may play a part in some way, we don't fully understand how. However, what is understood is that trauma, specifically childhood trauma, is linked to the development of schizophrenia.[5] This example stresses the importance of understanding childhood trauma and how it interacts with mental health disorders. Simply stating the biomedical model as the reason for mental health disorders leads to impeding this understanding and, in my opinion, causes pervasive struggles for those struggling with mental health diagnoses. We need to understand why the chemical imbalance or structural differences may be occurring, and one clear answer appears to be trauma.

I believe genetics plays a role in mental health disorders, but not in the way most people assume. Personality and how an individual views the world are also significant factors in complex ways. I've noticed that many people who develop depressive disorders have incredibly deep minds, viewing the world through a profound lens. I think this depth is an inherent part of who they are, and at times, it becomes overwhelming, given how the world operates and how they are made to feel about their perspective. Those with anxiety often deeply care about others and how they are feeling. People with obsessive-compulsive disorder (OCD) tend to be detail-oriented and driven to excel. Individuals with bipolar disorder are highly sensitive to their environment and the world around them. I believe these traits are a part of their identity, and at times, interacting with the world through such a unique lens can become challenging, possibly leading to the development of a disorder.

I like to view mental health disorders—as we categorize them in our culture—as struggles in how we interact with the world. Many of the diagnoses we label in our culture are rooted in shame and trauma. These disorders are not signs that something is inherently

Whenever we suppress our true selves, dysregulation and dysfunction follow.

wrong with you; they represent the challenges you face while navigating a world built on rigid systems and ways of functioning. Whenever we suppress our true selves, dysregulation and dysfunction follow. Untreated childhood trauma can present with a broad array of symptoms and mimic many other mental health diagnoses. In these cases, the diagnoses can be a part of the armor we wear, as we have to develop different adaptive strategies to avoid being hurt in the same ways we were previously. They are the adaptations that do not address the root cause of our suffering.

The Complex Truth

We begin adapting to our environment from the moment we are conceived. This is why when women are pregnant, they are given strict guidelines on what to ingest and how to care for their bodies during the pregnancy. In somatic therapy, our work can take us from processing something from a few days ago to processing something that occurred to us in utero or to our ancestors. I know how this sounds; when I first started this work, I could not believe that what we experienced in utero or something our ancestors experienced could impact our mental health and health throughout our lives, but it absolutely can. How? The answer is that all emotions and feelings are not just thoughts. They pulsate with the beat of your heart all the way through your body. They travel to every cell. They affect your genes.

A mother-to-be's body, undergoing extensive and consistent stress, whether due to a toxic home or work environment, will release stress hormones. These hormones permeate her body and impact every cell, including the fetus. I have helped many individuals process fear that they can't link to an event with a cognitive memory. By applying specific methods (some of which I describe later), they will access a fear like, "I am going to die." Through processing, they understand that this is such a young fear response, and many times, they can link it to a time when they were "very, very young," even in utero. Your brain starts storing information in utero, even if you cannot cognitively call on this information as readily as you can recall what you ate for lunch yesterday.

A study in 2020 found that basic memory traces are formed in utero and affect the automatic and neural reactions.[6] When my clients learn this, they deeply sigh, "So, you are saying that I was doomed from the start." "No, what I am saying is that you were and are a growing human being, and your environment impacted you from the moment you began to develop. Nothing was or is broken; you were merely adapting from the moment you came to be, and sometimes, this adaptation is not helpful or relevant in your current life."

This level of vulnerability can be frightening. We do not control much of what goes on in our minds and bodies because they operate on an automatic system. Most of the literature I have read suggests that we are 5–10 percent conscious of our actions, thoughts, and feelings. That means 90–95 percent of what happens within us is unconscious and automatic. Our emotional impulses are mostly unconscious, and then, we are shamed for them. My work has been to help individuals create safe and healthy ways to follow and allow for these impulses so they don't lose control of them later.

The complex truth here is that every cell in your body is trying to evolve and adapt with the goal of survival; the brain is no different. The brain is an adaptive organ and is never trying to cause harm. Therefore, many of the mental health diagnoses we treat in the mental health field are maladaptive adaptations that the brain undergoes in response to the world around us. This adaptation is most likely to occur in childhood because our brains are rapidly developing and most of our brain's learning occurs during this period, making childhood trauma an extremely strong contributor to most mental health conditions.

The root of childhood trauma often lies in the belief that something is fundamentally wrong with who we are—that the way we exist in the world is somehow flawed, or that we, as individuals, are inherently deficient. This belief fosters immense shame, which becomes the foundation of childhood trauma and Complex Post-Traumatic Stress Disorder (CPTSD). The truth is that every individual is unique. We each have diverse needs, cognitive processes, and distinct ways of perceiving the world. Our brains function differently, and when our parents cannot understand how we interact with them and the world, they may inadvertently or intentionally shame us. This can happen in cases of physical or verbal abuse, or through neglect and more subtle forms of emotional abuse, all of which contribute to childhood trauma.

The armoring patterns discussed throughout this book are linked to the ways we try to power through life to conceal the parts of ourselves we believe are flawed due to childhood trauma. For example, if we believe our very existence is flawed, we may develop the armoring pattern of elusiveness. If we believe that needing others is our flaw, we may adopt the armoring pattern of the Need Armor. If we believe that seeking joy and pleasure from life by asserting our autonomy is wrong, we may develop Endurance Armor. If we think losing control of ourselves or our emotions makes us less lovable, we may develop the armoring pattern of the one who craves control, Control Armor. And if we believe that seeking autonomy makes us less lovable, we may develop the armoring pattern of the one who strives for perfection, or Perfection Armor.

Again, these armoring patterns are unconscious ways of masking who we are to be more acceptable to the world around us. We therapists are treating the shame that leads to the masking, and we are using somatic healing to unveil some of the individuals' true selves. For instance, the goal of therapy is not to make the wearer of Need Armor need less. Instead, the goal is to help them embrace their needs and interact with the part of them that needs in a way that feels authentic and healthy to them. For the one wearing Control Armor, the goal is to help them learn that they are still lovable, even if they lose control.

As mentioned previously, your brain is constantly and consistently trying to adapt to the individual battles you face. It is trying to protect and carry you through difficult situations. We all face battles based on factors outside of ourselves that we cannot control. We can't control which families we are born into or what income level or class. We can't control whether a loved one dies or if we will experience a life-changing accident. We can't control our race, ethnicity, or sexuality. These factors have huge implications on the trauma we may face and the armor we may develop and carry throughout our lives.

Childhood is a crucial part of our psychological development because it shapes our present life and future. I know this from personal experience, professional experience, and many years of studying scientific research. This can be easily understood just based on what we know about the brain's function. Our brain stores memories in the form of neural connections and pathways. Neural pathways are the intricate networks of connections between neurons in the brain that form the foundation of our thoughts, behaviors, and emotional responses. An inverse relationship exists between age and neural connections being built during these years; the younger we are, the more neural connections we build, and vice versa. By 25 years old, nearly all of our neural connections are built and wired into our brains.

This demonstrates the importance of the learning we experience during these younger years. That learning gets hard-wired into our brains during the first 25 years of our lives. Trauma can disrupt the neural connections being built, creating patterns of fear, stress, and negative memories that become deeply ingrained in our neural circuitry. We know that these pathways are designed to be stored, so that we may utilize this learning and knowledge for future events. However, what is stored in the circumstances of adapting to childhood trauma is later maladaptive, even if, at one point, it was adaptive.

Basically, the brain is a giant sorting machine of information. It takes situations, asking if this is a new or old situation. If it is new, it utilizes the brain's problem-solving part to identify what to do. There is no reactiveness or previously stored bias. If the brain deems a to be known, it fires up the circuit of neural pathways containing the memories and knowledge utilized last time. I share all this to scientifically validate the idea of childhood trauma and explain why many therapists focus so much on childhood. However, it is important not to become disheartened by the science. Although our brain is wired by the time we're 25, we can still adjust and shift the wiring. The brain is remarkably plastic, so it can reorganize previous learning and, based on new experiences, strengthen new connections and weaken old connections.

Mental health disorders are not simply biological; they are deeply shaped by a person's psychological experiences, especially those from childhood and young adult years. As mentioned earlier, they are also shaped by our cognitive processes and how we naturally interact with the world. Psychological theories emphasize the importance of life events, personal history, and cognitive patterns in the development and perpetuation of mental health issues. I cannot tell you the number of people who feel broken and confused, and believe that their latest mental health diagnosis is a life sentence, which implies yet another way in which they are broken or flawed. This way of thinking about mental health can be dangerous. A diagnosis is simply a label given based on symptoms presented. It is not an identity.

A diagnosis is simply a label given based on symptoms presented. It is not an identity.

Our western medical model has designed a system that encourages us to believe our body is flawed and works against us. This system creates resentment toward ourselves and even our treatment approaches. We learn to work against our bodies and our realities rather than learning to work with them. We are ashamed of our brain's wiring rather than working to understand it. We spend much of our energy resisting, not in reprocessing and working on accepting ourselves as we are. I am here to say, I think the systems we exist in are flawed and work against us.

If we want to improve mental health without requiring individuals to don armor, we must shift our entire system. We are overworked, overstressed, and over-pressured to perform, and our basic needs for healthcare, financial stability, and even our ability to buy food may face threats. Our autonomy is threatened, if not at home, by how we are told to act, think, and learn through overly prescriptive systems of education, occupation, healthcare, and media. No wonder we live in a world of mental health disorders and trauma.

Eating disorders are a great example of how society interacts with our mental health and influences the expression of mental health disorders. Someone with an eating disorder may have other family members with an eating disorder. Genetics may be a factor, but not a clear one. Epigenetics is the most likely genetic factor here. What is apparent is that most individuals with eating disorders have experienced some trauma. We even have patterns of the type of trauma experienced and the type of eating disorder developed. One common underlying trauma of eating disorders is the belief that they are unlovable. Their brain tries to find solutions, taking in information on what makes someone lovable. It latches onto societal views, which tell individuals they are more lovable if they look a certain way. Their brain undergoes restructuring, neural formation, and rewiring, which creates an unconscious drive for survival, one that involves an eating disorder. This drive for survival can, coincidentally, lead to death.

The brain is a complex organ and utilizes 20 percent of our oxygen consumption, but accounts for only 5 percent of our mass. It operates every system in our body, either consciously or unconsciously. The heart does not act alone to keep us alive; it is the brain. Without the brain, the heart would not beat.

The myth that your brain is chemically broken, and therefore, you have depression or another disorder, simplifies an overly complex reality and can be dangerous.

No two people's brains are the same. The chemical composition and the neural connections of our brains are as different as each individual's personality and human experience. This means no two people experience the world in the same way, even if they have the same mental health diagnosis.

Evolutionarily speaking, the idea that our brain has remained in the same condition doesn't make sense. Whether that condition is classified as depression, anxiety, trauma disorders, or so on, your brain is an adaptive organ. It wants to heal and regenerate, and ultimately, is always working toward survival and homeostasis. Therefore, any flaw in the brain's system is an obvious learning and adaptation, flawed or not, to environmental stimuli. The brain is never the same, not even from one moment to the next; it is ever-changing.

It is essential to determine what caused our brains to develop these negative symptoms. What is causing us to struggle so intensely? If our brain is not healing itself, it is not broken; it is missing what it needs to heal. One year, I planted a garden and grew tomatoes. The tomato plants grew. They were beautiful, but as they ripened, they became misshapen. Of course, I became angry at the tomato plant for not giving me healthy, well-rounded tomatoes after all my hard work. However, upon reflection and some humility check-ins, I decided to research what I could have done better. This was my first time growing tomatoes, and maybe I was the one who caused their malformation. Maybe the tomatoes weren't at fault. I discovered that this is a common

> **If our brain is not healing itself, it is not broken; it is missing what it needs to heal.**

problem when the soil lacks certain nutrients. Once I gave the soil what it needed, healthy tomatoes flourished.

We need to be provided with the conditions that allow us to work toward healing, including meeting basic safety needs, such as food, water, and shelter. It often also involves medications and medical support to create an environment conducive to new learning. Additionally, it requires being in an environment of unconditional safety and belonging—a sense of security that, for many, may not be fully experienced until they step into a therapist's office.

The clients I see most often have been in therapy before and received some benefit. However, they still feel confused and defeated, wondering if anything will bring them relief. Many have been seeking care for medical conditions and were sent to therapy due to not being able to find an underlying cause for their chronic gastrointestinal issues or chronic pain. They usually have several diagnoses—anxiety, depression, or bipolar disorder—and have been treated for many years with minimal benefit or a good amount of benefit, yet they feel something is missing.

They have Complex Post-Traumatic Stress Disorder underlying their original diagnosis and need trauma treatment. When one of these individuals enters my office, I promise to walk with them into places of their mind they don't know, understand, or even have conscious memories of. Their multiple diagnoses look like a haphazard jumble of words to explain every symptom that presents, rather than helping the person understand how to address the root problem.

This system is flawed. We take a symptom of a person's need for structure or a person who experiences mood fluctuations and assume this is a flaw within them, rather than recognizing this symptom is an adaptation they made to an environmental situation. This system creates a passive helplessness in their treatment. Rather than helping them understand how their brain interacts with the environment around them and, in stressful situations, will lead to the negative symptoms defined in a mental health disorder, we assume their diagnosis indicates something is wrong with their brain.

A diagnosis often describes how your brain is currently functioning and how it may function in the future if overwhelmed. People growing up in traumatic environments have entirely different chemical baselines than others, even if their brains are physiologically the same. For such an individual, the brain is in a constant state of hyperarousal, so the threshold for stress is lower than for those without trauma. This state leads to an increased use of adaptive strategies related to many of the mental health diagnoses we see: depression, anxiety, personality disorders, and disorders related to emotional dysregulation. For this reason, individuals with trauma are significantly more likely to be diagnosed with a mental health disorder.

The Genetic Component of Armor Formation

A vital factor in armor selection is the battles that lie ahead. This is where genetics becomes important, but not in the way you may think. The field of epigenetics has opened up new pathways for understanding how our environment and life experiences influence mental health throughout generations. While our genes provide the basic blueprint for who we are, the epigenome determines which genes are activated or silenced in response to external factors. These changes can significantly impact the brain, influencing how we think, feel, and react to stress and adversity.

One of the most profound ways epigenetics influences mental health is through stress. Chronic stress—whether from childhood adversity, trauma, or prolonged emotional strain—can lead to lasting epigenetic changes in the brain. These changes can affect the expression of genes involved in regulating mood and stress response, such as those responsible for producing stress hormones like cortisol. Over time, these modifications can increase vulnerability to mental health conditions like depression, anxiety, and post-traumatic stress disorder. Due to CPTSD being pervasive and involving sustained and repeated exposure to trauma, people with this condition undergo a shift in the expression of genes, possibly leading to the expression of genes associated with other mental health disorders.

Epigenetic changes can also affect how we process emotions and form memories. In the brain, these modifications can affect neuroplasticity—the brain's ability to reorganize itself by forming new neural connections. For example, environmental factors may turn on or off specific genes involved in synaptic function and communication between brain cells, impacting cognitive abilities and emotional regulation. A well-known example is the role of epigenetics in depression, where alterations in the expression of genes that regulate synaptic plasticity may impair mood regulation and resilience.

Furthermore, epigenetic modifications can be inherited, meaning the mental health of one generation can influence the next. For instance, if a parent experiences significant stress or mental illness, they may pass down epigenetic markers to their offspring, increasing the likelihood of similar conditions arising, even in the absence of genetic mutations. This inheritance of epigenetic changes offers a potential explanation for the intergenerational transmission of mental health disorders, making it clear that genetics and environment work together in complex ways to shape mental well-being.

A notable research study, "Transgenerational Effects of Trauma in Rats: A Model for the Study of Epigenetic Mechanisms in Intergenerational Transmission of Trauma," explored how a generation of rats could transmit their trauma to subsequent generations through epigenetic mechanisms.[7] In this study, female rats were exposed to early-life stress (such as maternal separation), and their offspring exhibited behavioral changes, including heightened anxiety and altered stress responses. Researchers found that these offspring had a reduction in the expression of a gene crucial for regulating the stress hormone cortisol. Most notably, the second-generation offspring, not directly exposed to the trauma, also displayed similar stress-related behaviors and gene expression changes, suggesting that trauma effects could be inherited through epigenetic modifications.

This study provided significant evidence that trauma can affect not only the individuals who directly experience it but also their descendants, potentially through epigenetic mechanisms like DNA methylation, which alter gene expression without changing the underlying genetic code. This research has important implications for understanding the biological transmission of trauma in humans, especially in the context of intergenerational trauma.

What makes epigenetics particularly compelling is its potential for intervention. While we cannot change our genetic code, epigenetic modifications are dynamic and reversible. It may be possible to reverse harmful epigenetic changes and promote better physical and mental health outcomes through lifestyle changes, such as a balanced diet, regular exercise, mindfulness practices, or therapeutic interventions like psychotherapy. This emerging knowledge offers hope for personalized approaches to mental health care.

CHAPTER 3

THE DIFFERENT ARMOR WE WEAR

The body carries the weight of our history.
—Dr. Alexander Lowen

Imagine your inner child, the part of you full of vigor, vulnerability, freedom, and sensitivity—the carrier of your pain and your excitement. This inner child is the vulnerable and messy part of you who doesn't always know what to do but wears their heart on their sleeve. In front of them stands a soldier, the part tasked with protecting and keeping safe the vulnerable parts of the person. This part of you has built armor specifically designed to protect the unique you. Once in a while, the inner child peeks out around the soldier and sees life ahead, but the soldier quickly reminds them to stay back; it isn't safe out there. Remember how much it hurt to be vulnerable and exposed when you were young? Your inner child desires to be free, but tucks back behind the soldier because safety is more important than freedom.

This soldier has a chip on their shoulder. They have promised never to let what hurt us previously hurt us again. This activates defense mechanisms that we unknowingly carry. We don't even remember what it is like to live without the soldier part of us anymore. We have become hypervigilant, ready to defend ourselves and fight to find a space of safety where we can breathe. Unfortunately, we have no idea what that even means anymore. We are in the midst of a war that commandeers our lives—a war for safety rather than one of connection, joy, and peace.

The armor of childhood trauma related to the diagnosis of complex post-traumatic stress disorder is defense patterns designed to protect us from being harmed. The armor is the pattern of stress in our body, emotional defenses, and patterns of how we interact with others. The armor comprises the symptoms that give us the diagnosis of complex post-traumatic stress disorder. The definition of armor is the same for all of us, but the armor we carry is different for every individual I have met.

However, there are patterns and mechanisms to help us understand ourselves. Many factors dictate the armor we choose: the trauma we face, our genetics, and other individualized factors we will not understand until we go through psychotherapy. One thing is certain: the armor we carry is perfectly selected by our mind and body to carry us through life's difficulties. Our body and mind continually work to help us evolve, adapt, and survive. Remember, mental health disorders are flawed adaptive strategies rather than an attack or malfunction of the brain.

> **Our body and mind continually work to help us evolve, adapt, and survive.**

Why We Don Armor

Trauma, particularly when experienced chronically or at a young age, can significantly affect the body, often manifesting in muscle tension, postural changes, and physical discomfort. When the body is exposed to trauma, especially in the form of stress or abuse, the nervous system can enter a state of heightened alertness—the "fight, flight, or freeze" mode—causing muscles to contract and remain tense for extended periods. Your body actually begins to brace itself in defense. This prolonged tension can lead to stiffness, pain, and discomfort in the neck, shoulders, jaw, and back. Over time, these muscles restructure themselves, like building muscles through lifting weights. They then may become fatigued, weaker, or more prone to injury.

One study that explores the connection between trauma and physical health is Van der Kolk's book *Trauma and Memory: Brain and Body in a Search for the Living Past*.[8] This research emphasizes how traumatic experiences impact the body by triggering a constant state of stress, which affects the musculoskeletal system. Van der Kolk explains that trauma activates the body's "fight, flight, or freeze" response, leading to sustained muscle tension as the body remains in a hyper-aroused state. The study demonstrated that this sustained state can contribute to chronic muscle pain, tension, and postural issues, particularly in the neck, back, and shoulders.

The study also discusses how trauma can cause changes in the nervous system that affect the body's ability to relax, contributing to physical manifestations like poor posture and discomfort. These physical changes often persist unless therapeutic intervention addresses both the mind and body, demonstrating the profound connection between psychological and physical health. This research underscores the importance of integrating somatic trauma-informed care in healing, recognizing that trauma affects the mind but also the physical form.

When we experience trauma, our brain is functioning as it is supposed to, by developing Post-Traumatic Stress Disorder or Complex Post-Traumatic Stress Disorder. Unfortunately, adapting to unsafe environments means developing post-traumatic stress symptoms.

The Body's Armor

"The body does not lie. Even when a person tries to hide his true feelings by some sort of artificial postural attitude, his body believes the pose in the state of tension that is created."⁹ This quote powerfully captures why some clients appear deeply disconnected from their bodies—and, as a result, from their emotions. Rather than living their truth, they are often trying to construct one, following patterns they've learned for self-protection. In response, the body works to support this internal narrative, building tension and creating muscular armor to shield the vulnerability they were taught to hide. Our body becomes armor to protect and carry us through the next battle. It becomes less graceful and more functional.

Trauma affects the body in ways that can lead to chronic conditions and long-term health problems. The physiological mechanisms underlying these effects primarily involve the nervous, endocrine, and immune systems. The body's acute stress response, the "fight, flight, or freeze" response, is a natural reaction to perceived danger. When faced with a threat, the brain activates the hypothalamic-pituitary-adrenal (HPA) axis, releasing hormones, such as cortisol and adrenaline, to prepare the body for immediate action. While this response is adaptive in the short-term situations for which it is intended, prolonged activation of the stress system can detrimentally affect physical and mental health.

> **The body's acute stress response, often referred to as the "fight, flight, or freeze" response, is a natural reaction to perceived danger.**

Research shows that individuals with a history of trauma, particularly chronic trauma, such as childhood abuse or repeated exposure to stressors, have a dysregulated stress response. Heim demonstrated that individuals with a history of childhood trauma, particularly those with PTSD or CPTSD, exhibit heightened cortisol levels and abnormal HPA axis functioning, even in the absence of immediate stressors.[10] The HPA axis is an important part of how we respond to and regulate stress. Abnormal functioning of the HPA axis can lead to chronic stress and a malfunctioning stress response system, which are linked to a variety of physical health problems, including cardiovascular disease, diabetes, and autoimmune disorders, demonstrating the link between mental health and physical health.

Similarly, Kendall-Tackett found that trauma survivors are more likely to develop chronic pain syndromes, such as fibromyalgia, and gastrointestinal disorders, including irritable bowel syndrome (IBS).[11] A combination of altered brain chemistry and a hyperactive immune response is the mechanism leading to inflammation and physical symptoms.

Trauma exposure is also linked to an increased risk of chronic illness across an individual's lifespan. The ACE study, a large-scale investigation into childhood trauma and adult health outcomes, demonstrated a robust connection between childhood trauma and a variety of chronic physical conditions. Felitti found that individuals with high ACE scores (indicating significant early-life trauma) were more likely to experience chronic diseases, such as heart disease, stroke, diabetes, and cancer as adults.[12] Continual exposure to trauma has a profound impact on the immune system, often leading to a hyper-inflammatory response.

Bower found that individuals with PTSD had elevated levels of pro-inflammatory cytokines, molecules that promote inflammation in the body.[13] This heightened inflammatory response has been implicated in the development of numerous conditions, including rheumatoid arthritis, asthma, and cardiovascular disease. These studies, and many more, demonstrate empirically that trauma affects the mind and body of the individual who endures it and that trauma continues to affect the body throughout a lifetime until treated.

Throughout the years, clients have asked how trauma impacts their entire body. The answer is complex and involves biological and behavioral mechanisms. Trauma can lead to unhealthy survival strategies, such as smoking, overeating, and substance abuse, which increase the risk of chronic conditions. Additionally, trauma-induced dysregulation of the immune system can result in chronic inflammation, a contributor to the development of many diseases.

When someone enters my office, I observe how their body holds their story. I sit with them and breathe while allowing my body to react to theirs. I do this because our body has its own language that we must learn to listen to. Our body is evolutionarily designed to take in information and respond physiologically without thinking. If you let it, your body will give you a wealth of information. That is why you instantly feel safe when you walk into some rooms, while in others, you feel a tightness in your chest or tingling in your arms. Your body is picking up on information that your thinking brain is missing and responding through the language of feeling, your body's wisdom, or intuition.

For example, if I am with someone who tends to be dissociative, I will sense a fear response in my body and, usually, a little pressure in my head. If I am with someone in a great deal of need, I may feel slightly overwhelmed initially. This is powerful information for several reasons. First, I do not want to utilize my body's unconscious response system against the client. I want to take it in as information and remind my body that I am safe because I am here to help this individual with this particular issue. I will use this information during bodywork with the client to process the issues that are presented, which gives their body and mine the opportunity to process these feelings.

When individuals first come through my door, they are often frustrated and tired of their body protecting them. As they process this frustration, I often feel gratitude that we do not have all the control over our unconscious response; otherwise, many of us wouldn't still be alive. We would not have been able to endure the trauma we suffered. As clients do their therapeutic work, I see their bodies relax and become graceful and at peace, leaving behind the armor's stiffness.

Imagine noticing emotion as it builds in your body. Imagine recognizing and utilizing this rather than accepting it as a part of your body in the form of tension. Many of us fight the discomfort and don't understand that it is fighting on our behalf. The body wants to be free, but the trauma it carries won't let it lay down the armor. It fascinates and inspires me to see my clients' bodies and minds step in unconsciously to protect and save them from difficult situations and set them free when they learn to follow.

> **The body wants to be free, but the trauma it carries won't let it lay down the armor.**

Many individuals with childhood trauma or adverse childhood experiences have specific defense mechanisms depending on their experience and the age of the experience. Lowen described the body's armor through "character structures" based on some of the most common armoring patterns.[14] These defensive patterns have specific characteristics that may be seen physically in the body and discussed emotionally due to the individual's consistent struggles and behavioral patterns. While I think this is mostly accurate, I also believe it could be incomplete in some cases. Children face distinct challenges at different stages. For instance, an infant or fetus needs to feel wanted to feel safe; a baby requires a sense of safety through nourishment and nurturing; and an older child needs the security of boundaries and the freedom to express themselves. This is why age matters—childhood trauma can lead to specific armoring patterns, depending on the developmental stage.

However, I also believe that a child, regardless of age, who consistently feels unwanted can still develop an armoring pattern similar to that of a fetus or infant, even if this occurs after infancy. Similarly, a child who struggles with feeling nurtured could develop this character structure at any age. In theory, the severity of armoring may be lessened and the physiological effects may be reduced, but the armoring may still be present. This underscores the idea that parents can mitigate the effects of trauma by adjusting their behaviors and narratives at any stage of development, potentially lessening the long-term impact on the child. It is also important to note that armor can develop from a child's perspective of a situation if the situation is not processed, even if the perspective is not true.

Later in the book, I will describe a client who developed an armoring pattern following her father's mental health struggles and death. She perceived that, due to her developmental stage and ability to process the situation, her father rejected her, although that was not meant to be the case. Her family never spoke of the struggles of her father, so she processed and stored this experience as rejection and armoring ensued.

Recognizing these armoring patterns has helped me understand how to direct a client's therapy. They allow me to explore which emotions the individual may need to express and in what order.

The Energetic Armoring

Trauma can significantly impact a person's energy, encompassing physical vitality and emotional well-being. Frequently, it results in heightened stress responses, activating the body's fight, flight, or freeze mechanisms, which drain energy over time. Research indicates that individuals with trauma histories often experience chronic fatigue, sleep disturbances, and emotional exhaustion due to the continuous physiological stress response.[15] Studies have also shown that trauma can disrupt the balance of the autonomic nervous system, leading to dysregulation in energy levels.[16] Furthermore, trauma's effect on the brain, particularly in areas related to emotional regulation, contributes to an ongoing sense of depletion, making it harder for individuals to experience vitality or motivation.[17] Healing from trauma involves therapeutic practices, such as somatic therapies, to restore energy. These approaches aim to recalibrate the body's responses and foster energy restoration.

You can sense someone's energetic armor by being around them. You can look into their eyes and feel their level of energy. You can sit with them and notice how much energy their body releases. The amount of energy in their speech and aliveness in their body are important determinants of their energetic armoring. Someone who has experienced a lot in life can either have depleted or manic energy, depending on how the energy chooses to armor itself.

As I sit with someone, I notice how my body and energy feel in their presence. Some individuals pour out all their energy into the room for me. Others feel tired and far away, like I can't quite access them, even though they are in front of me. Whatever energy I feel, I consider that if I am feeling this energy, others in the client's life are too.

Sometimes, clients tell me, "I can't connect to people," "My friends think I am too needy," or "No one wants to be around me." In these situations, the client is acting in the opposite of this energy, so they can't understand why others respond in this way. For instance, the person needing a lot of reassurance will often act as if they don't need it, yet others still call them needy. The dissociated individual will be excessively friendly or compliant, but others will recognize that they aren't really present.

Our energy, much like the body, tells a story. For example, someone wearing Need Armor didn't get their needs met in their childhood. Or consider someone who has an energy of being depleted, most likely fights to survive every day, and has been doing this for a long time. Another may have angry energy because they weren't allowed to be angry as a child.

What we feel exuding from someone's presence will tell us some of the story of their trauma. To listen to this silent story, we must recognize that we do not just transfer information from our thinking brain. Much of the connection we experience is processed in the unconscious brain through the conduit of our bodies and intuition. Our body always projects and picks up on the truth. This makes individuals feel vulnerable as they begin their work with me because they learn they can't continue the façade forever. They learn that to have the life they want and deserve, they need to process their struggle and embrace their authentic self.

Often, their psychological armor tells us a story that is the opposite of the truth that their energetic story is presenting. Those who have a lot of needs tell themselves they need nothing. Those who need connection tell themselves they are happy to be alone. When we do this, we are not trying to be dishonest; we truly believe this. We are protecting ourselves from the discomfort of the fear that these needs will never actually be met—we are adapting.

Psychological Armoring

While the body responds to trauma, the mind processes these events in ways that can lead to lasting psychological effects.

Trauma's emotional and cognitive aftermath can manifest in a variety of mental health disorders, including PTSD, depression, anxiety, and dissociative disorders.

Earlier, I mentioned how we view the body and mind as separate entities. If you have high blood pressure, a doctor may tell you to manage your stress. Many individuals hear this as "stop letting things that stress you take up so much space in your brain." Unfortunately, we don't get to control through thinking what takes up space in our unconscious brain and therefore what emotions affect our physical health. Clients tell me that they have been told not to stress. Consequently, the conscious brain represses the stress and worsens the issue. Now, we are stressed, and we are denying our stress and leaving it unnoticed and unchecked.

Most individuals don't know how to reduce stress. It isn't as simple as denying that something is causing you stress; this is repression, not emotional regulation. Emotional repression may reduce the outward expression of emotion to the comfort of everyone else; however, it will not rid the body of the tension. To truly manage stress or any other emotion, we must become more aware of them. We must become painfully aware of how these emotions feel in our bodies and learn how to comfort them.

> **We must become painfully aware of how these emotions feel in our bodies and learn how to comfort them.**

Some providers will discuss your struggles with you to help you reframe thoughts and change your feelings. This works on the conscious brain but doesn't help the body process or regulate with its natural regulation system. Thoughts and reframing are important and helpful parts of a holistic treatment plan, but often something must be added to this approach. For example, if someone is struggling with physical manifestations that could be linked to stress on the body, such as ulcers, arthritis, gastrointestinal disease, or high blood pressure, they should seek treatment from a medical doctor. Also, they should seek a therapist to use somatic therapies to discharge the emotions that have caused stress on the body.

When someone comes to me with an "anger problem," I explain that they actually have a repression problem. Their anger doesn't need to be managed; it needs to be released in a healthy way, and then they can manage it. When you get angry, your jaw tightens, your shoulders raise, and your body releases chemicals to signal that a fight will ensue. When you convince yourself, using your 5 percent conscious brain, that you should not be angry, you may calm your conscious mind, but it doesn't prevent your body from feeling the anger. In time, the system will calm down, and you will stop feeling angry. However, now your system has changed. Your body stores this response, and the next time you get angry, it will be more prepared and trigger the physiological anger response more quickly.

The more you experience anger, the quicker-tempered you will become. The more shame you have about your anger, the more you will repress it. The more you repress your emotions, the more likely you are to have mental and physical consequences of the repression. This is a dangerous cycle of emotional repression.

Much like in physics, every action has an equal and opposite reaction in our brain. The more your conscious brain pushes against the anger to repress it, the stronger the anger response will push back and the more reactive you will be, which triggers your adaptive brain to fight for you and do what it knows to survive. The more this happens, the more you lose control of your anger.

Suppose you have worked through repressed anger and know your physiological cues for it. You feel your shoulders rise and your jaw tighten as a friend talks to you about something. Instead of ignoring the feeling, pause, take a deep breath, and let your body share its information with you. Your friend is saying something upsetting to you about a past event. You make a choice: share your feelings with your friend and set a gentle boundary, or breathe and comfort yourself with understanding and connection. The alternative is to consciously or subconsciously ignore the feeling. Your friend keeps talking. You get through the interaction, but the next time your friend discusses this, you can't ignore the feeling, so you begin to yell at your friend. This is a solid example of expression vs. repression. Soldiering through emotion through repression leads to disconnection, armoring, and, more than likely, explosive emotions later.

Doris came to me feeling depressed and having suicidal thoughts because she was unable to meet work requirements. As I began my normal intake, she instantly showed signs of being frustrated with my questions or lack of questions. She was angry with me even though she was coming to see me. She sounded cooperative and willing as she talked, but her body language told a different story.

"I just don't know why I can't get things done! I want to do well. I want to be successful. I wake up in the morning with a desire to please my boss and make him value me!" Her prefrontal cortex spoke.

"How do you feel when you wake up for work?" I rebutted.

"I just told you that! I feel motivated and like I want to do a good job."

"No, Doris. How do you feel in your body?"

After a pause, she admitted with tears in her eyes, "I don't know what you mean."

After a few sessions, Doris got back into her body and learned its sensations and what they mean. She acknowledged feeling dread when she woke up. She hated her boss and her job. She felt her boss asked too much of her and didn't feel she could take it anymore. We processed all of this and, later, began to process her body's story.

Doris grew up with a domineering mother. Her mother loved her but expected her to act a certain way and be grateful for everything she did for her. Frequently, Doris heard her mother say, "Listen to me and don't get mad. You shouldn't feel mad at me." If Doris made a mistake, her mother would either withdraw love or lash out in anger. Doris learned to be a good girl, which is all she ever wanted to be. So, she set out into her life, graduating at the top of her high school class. Later, she struggled in college but managed to graduate. She entered a field where success only took hard work and endurance, something Doris knew well. She kept pushing and enduring until she couldn't. Now, she can't force herself to submit a work project on time. She is overeating to get herself to do things she doesn't want to do. She is in a marriage where she carries most of the load for childcare and household chores while being the primary breadwinner.

She is killing it, or is it killing her?

At times, Doris cried as she recounted her fate. She allowed herself to feel the sadness and defeat when I prompted her to breathe and feel. Sometimes, she would talk herself into pushing harder and continuing to work. We began our work with the breathing stool. After a while, she screamed in fury, and we moved to release her anger. Doris would hit the cube and yell, "I can't do it!" and "I don't want to!"

Eventually, anger stopped permeating our interactions, and she became easier to talk to. She started telling me what she would and wouldn't do in sessions and began to have healthy autonomy and set boundaries. She did her work with ease, recognizing that she was choosing to do the work; she wasn't forced or trapped and could leave at any time. She started to set boundaries with her husband, who was excited to receive them because he no longer felt the disdain from her. She began to ask for what she needed.

I am not suggesting that we react aggressively to every situation in which we get angry. This is not recommended.

When people come to me, they have so much stored anger that when we open the valve, we need to release it in a significant way in a safe space where the individual can become dysregulated; the therapist is present to keep them safe. In addition to therapy, we normalize emotions as a natural, automatic physiological response and create normalized methods of regulation for ourselves that involve our mind and body together. Much like when we are tired, we rest, or when we are hungry, we eat.

Similar to repressing emotions, when you are hungry, you can repress your hunger with your prefrontal cortex until you genuinely do not feel the hunger sensations. However, as soon as you are around something delicious again or take a bite of something, your unconscious brain takes over, overwhelming you with hunger again. This is why many individuals with restrictive eating disorders also struggle with binge eating or similar indulgent eating behaviors. The healthier alternative to repressing your hunger is listening to your stomach and using your prefrontal cortex to decide which food is best. Do you need comfort food or something healthy? What's best in this moment of hunger?

Emotional expression is how our body digests emotional experiences, much like our digestive system needs to digest food. If we interfere with this digestion process that our body naturally knows to do, we will lose control of its function, and dysregulation will ensue.

To begin to treat emotions, I propose we ask ourselves a series of questions when we notice an emotion:

- What does my body need from me at this moment?
- Does it need me to confront someone assertively?
- Does it need me to set a boundary?
- Does it need a good cry?

- Does it need a physical release, and if so, what is the best way to make that happen?

We must learn to listen to our emotions like any other critical regulatory function and utilize healthy releases, not repressive mechanisms, to create mental and physical well-being.

Once you repress an emotion, you are more easily brought to that emotion later, be it anger, sadness, guilt, or shame. When we are angry, we need to normalize safe and healthy somatic expression, whether that is scribbling our frustration on paper, hitting our bed for a while, or tensing our muscles and releasing them a few times. Suppose we are angry enough that we feel a physiological desire to fight. In that case, we need to allow our body to feel the release of a safe and healthy discharge so it will not store the anger and create emotional and perhaps physical issues later on.

What makes emotions different from hunger or thirst is the immense shame that comes with them. It has become a common belief that those who can't control their emotions lack control and are ill, unpredictable, or unstable. In actuality, they have had too much control and likely not enough comfort and teaching from primary caregivers to help them navigate emotions.

We potty train children and teach them to speak and eat, but too often, we do not teach them to regulate their emotions.

We potty train children and teach them to speak and eat, but too often, we do not teach them to regulate their emotions. This is because we are all victims of the emotional repression epidemic.

We have been taught to repress emotions for generations. When our children start to demonstrate emotion, we are triggered because we don't know how to help them, believe we do when we don't, or they trigger our own fear related to showing emotion. We respond by belittling them, telling them to calm down (they would if they could), or we send them to their room to sort it out on their own. We wouldn't make our kids figure out how and what to eat or how to use the bathroom without our guidance and support, and we shouldn't expect them to know how to utilize their emotions. If a child is acting violently, they are not violent children; they need redirection, not repression.

To further demonstrate the mind and body interweave, we can continue to utilize the common example of stress. We should teach our children much like we need to teach ourselves. Do you need to scream? Let's go outside and scream. Do you need to hit something? Please hit this pillow or twist this towel. Do you feel like crying? I am here to hold you and tell you everything is going to be okay. If you do this, they will be regulated. They will calm down. The next time they get angry or sad, they won't lose control. Their brain will be wired for healthy emotional regulation through safe emotional expression. This behavior will become natural and organic to them.

I have discussed how emotions are not just "in your head;" they live throughout your body. A great example of this is the condition known as *takotsubo cardiomyopathy*, more commonly known as broken heart syndrome. This syndrome is a temporary but severe disorder that occurs when someone is overcome with grief. Their heart structure is affected; the left ventricle is weakened. The heart literally changes shape to resemble a Japanese pot, the takotsubo. Individuals with this condition experience symptoms similar to a heart attack. Once they process the grief or time goes by, and the grief subsides, the individual's heart and function will return to normal. This demonstrates the effect emotions have on our body structure and function.

We know that emotional stress worsens arthritis, can cause and aggravate ulcers, heart disease, and a variety of physical health conditions. Yet, most individuals hear they need to "manage their stress," but are given no information on what that means. Why is the person stressed to the extent that it causes physical distress? I will argue again that the individual doesn't have a stress problem; they have an emotional repression problem. Our society uses *stress* to describe every possible emotion. We wear this widely accepted term like a badge of honor. To be stressed is to be busy, which means we are important and active.

However, stress is a physiological response to something deeper that we must understand. The body's stress response is designed to combat threats. You need to know why your daily life threatens you. Most commonly, this comes from the internal threat of shame. If individuals don't feel they are meeting some perceived or actual internal or external expectation, this can lead to a feeling of shame that threatens their worthiness. People must address that shame before they can truly manage their stress. No amount of coping techniques, deep breathing techniques, meditation, exercise, or any other of the repressive coping techniques will reduce their stress long term. It may just temporarily reduce their stress response, but this is like taking an aspirin for a severed finger. As soon as the pain receptors are able, they will start screaming for help once again. The stress response is your body's way of signaling something is wrong; to numb it without addressing the actual threat dishonors your body and the biological mechanism it has to try to help you. You cannot "cope" away trauma; you must heal it.

Often, I have encountered clients who request "techniques" to fix what is going on. However, when I provide techniques to lower their stress response, they become defensive or angry, saying, "I tried that; it doesn't work" or "Nothing helps." Truthfully, most of us don't want a "fix" to our struggles; we want someone to sit and partner with us

You cannot "cope" away trauma; you must heal it.

in our healing and regulation. As children, this is what was missing for most of us.

Trauma profoundly impacts how we think by altering our cognitive processes, memory, and perception of the world. After experiencing trauma, especially chronic or severe trauma, our brain stress response system becomes overactivated, often leading to difficulties in concentration, decision-making, and problem-solving. The emotional intensity of traumatic events can overwhelm the brain's ability to process and store memories coherently, which causes us to have fragmented or intrusive thoughts about the event. Eventually, this disruption can lead to us having persistent negative beliefs about ourselves, others, or the world, often manifesting as feelings of guilt, shame, or a sense of being unsafe. These are all the brain's attempts to adapt to the trauma. We unconsciously create beliefs to try to make the trauma easier to understand, but oftentimes, these beliefs make our lives more difficult in the long run.

Trauma can also impair the brain's ability to differentiate between past and present threats, causing hypervigilance or a constant state of alertness, even in non-threatening situations. Cognitive distortions, such as catastrophizing or black-and-white thinking, are also common in trauma survivors; they may interpret everyday experiences through a lens of fear or helplessness. Trauma makes it difficult for individuals to think clearly or process information rationally because the emotional impact overrides logical reasoning.

Many researchers have studied trauma and how it affects the function of the brain, including emotional regulation, memory recall, and formation. Their research demonstrated that trauma disrupts the brain's ability to process and integrate emotional memories, leading to significant changes in cognition and perception. It also showed that individuals suffering from PTSD often experience fragmented or dissociative thinking, where they may have difficulty recalling traumatic events in a coherent narrative, or they might experience intense emotional responses to reminders of the trauma. This disruption occurs primarily due to changes in several areas of the brain, including the hippocampus, which is responsible for memory consolidation, and the prefrontal cortex, which helps with emotional regulation and decision-making. Trauma impairs their ability to differentiate between past and present threats, leading to hypervigilance. This research emphasizes that these cognitive shifts can make it harder for trauma survivors to function effectively in daily life, as their thinking becomes more dominated by fear-based responses rather than rational thought.[18]

Trauma impacts how we view the world and the neural connections it has led to. We begin to view the world based on the roadmap stored in the neural pathways of our brain. The brain constantly uses these road maps to weed out any unknowns, creating narratives about what is occurring. Often, these narratives are rooted in our traumas, bringing the past into the present.

Suppose we grew up in an environment where resources such as food, water, or love and belonging were lacking. In such an environment, we will have a fear of scarcity rooted in our gut, even if those resources are no longer scarce. We see this in individuals who experience a lot of jealousy. They grew up in environments where attention, love, and connection seemed scarce. Their neural pathways created a story about that scarcity, and now, in connection with others, they feel the need to compete for a person's attention and love, even when there is no competition.

Psychological armor is designed to avoid feeling at all costs because emotions have become the enemy in the mind. The mind believes emotions are bad and/or dangerous, rather than just a natural regulatory system of the body. Often, this psychological armoring is automatic, practiced, and completely subconscious. Like driving home from work, you don't have to think about where you are going because your brain recognizes it has been here before. Psychological armoring causes us to find ourselves in the same situations repeatedly because we are subconsciously involved in creating it. We are building the same set of circumstances over and over, trying to feel safe.

Relationship Armoring

Trauma also impacts relationships by shaping the way individuals connect, communicate, and trust others. Trauma survivors may struggle with emotional regulation, leading to heightened reactions to stress or perceived threats, which can cause misunderstandings or conflicts. Trust, often damaged by betrayal or loss, may be difficult to rebuild, leading to fear of vulnerability or intimacy. Survivors may also withdraw, isolate themselves, or become overly protective, inadvertently distancing themselves from loved ones. Conversely, they might develop anxious attachment styles, seeking constant reassurance or becoming overly dependent on others for emotional support. The effects of trauma create cycles of emotional distress, which make it challenging for individuals to maintain healthy, balanced relationships unless there is open communication, mutual understanding, and healing.

Relational trauma is especially difficult for relationships because relationships are the triggers. This kind of trauma, which arises from experiences of betrayal, abuse, neglect, or emotional harm within close relationships, has a lasting and deep impact on future connections. Individuals who have endured relational trauma may develop trust issues, fearing that loved ones could hurt or abandon them. This fear manifests in a variety of ways, such as emotional withdrawal, vulnerability, or an intense need for control to avoid further pain. Sometimes, people experience patterns of anxiety, jealousy, or codependency and often struggle to maintain healthy boundaries or differentiate between love and control. The emotional scars of relational trauma make it hard for a person to feel safe or valued in new relationships, leading to cycles of attachment issues, misunderstandings, or even re-enacting past trauma in ways that inadvertently replicate harmful dynamics. Healing from relational trauma requires deep self-awareness, therapy, and support, as well as cultivating trust and mutual respect in relationships. Using our analogy of soldiers, we see how relational trauma turns relationships into the primary war zone. Our early relationships were the initial trauma, so later relationships become the battleground where we work out much of our trauma.

Joe was experiencing OCD-like behaviors and difficulties in his relationships. He shared that he will spend several hours getting ready for the day. He ensures each hair lies perfectly and his complexion is flawless before leaving home. Throughout the day, he will check his appearance with a pocket mirror and go home if something doesn't meet his expectations. Joe struggles in relationships. He believes that if someone loves him, they will meet all his needs and never hurt him. If someone does hurt him, he ends the relationship without a second thought. As he talked, he appeared not to be breathing, although he must have been.

Healing from relational trauma requires deep self-awareness, therapy, and support, as well as cultivating trust and mutual respect in relationships.

A relationship with a therapist is just that, a relationship. So, the first thing I did with Joe was discuss the relationship issue because ours would be the next relationship on the chopping block. To be successful, we needed to successfully navigate conflict. We began processing his difficulties with being defensive. He shared the relationship offenses, which ranged from a lie to not considering him in their dinner plans to an argument where something hurtful was said. He acknowledged his struggle with perfectionism both within himself and with his partners. Joe is immensely lonely but believes it is safest to be alone because no one will hurt him.

My first job was to validate his belief about getting hurt. It is an unfortunate truth that we all get hurt in love and life. The ones who deserve our love despite hurting us are the ones who do it unknowingly and want to rectify the hurt by working on themselves and the relationships. I encouraged Joe to bioenergetically process his protest to this reality, which he declined to do initially but did in later sessions. So, what happened to Joe that he could no longer tolerate any hurt? It had significantly reduced his ability to live a rich life.

During processing, we discovered that his mother was extremely harsh with him. She rejected hugs from him for as long as he could remember and would pull away when he went to hold her hand or snuggle in close. His father died when he was young, and his mother never remarried. Life was just Joe and his mom, and from what Joe felt, his mom wanted it to be only her.

As he processed his story and we began getting him into his body, he exhaled more deeply, and with it came the grief locked within. Joe had been holding the grief of losing his father in his breath, and with his father's death, he also lost his mother. As we worked, his grief grew deeper and louder. He would yell out in despair. In time, he became more tolerant of imperfections in himself and his partners because his body began to trust that he could occasionally tolerate a little rejection; he had created emotional space for it. His body had been shielding him from rejection by becoming as perfect as possible and rejecting others at any sign of trouble before he could be rejected.

Before he did this work, I don't know that Joe could have tolerated further rejection. The OCD diagnosis and his seemingly cruel relationship strategies absolutely saved his life. He felt shame for these behaviors, but there was no better way for him to protect himself until he found a space and method to grieve. His body was brilliant, and he knew he could not withstand one more rejection, so it made sure he never had to.

Enneagram Comparison

Throughout this book, you will find at the end of a chapter a comparison of what Enneagram type may be associated with the defensive pattern described in the chapter. I did this because I believe the enneagram has some beautiful insights into a soldier's armoring and a unique perspective that many are finding helpful currently. The Enneagram is a personality typing system that identifies nine distinct types of people, each with their own core motivations, fears, and coping mechanisms. The theory suggests that these types are shaped by early life experiences and internal psychological drives, influencing how individuals perceive the world and relate to others. Each type has its strengths and weaknesses, and the Enneagram offers insights into how these patterns can evolve through self-awareness and growth. I believe this can be helpful to relate to the bioenergetic armoring patterns because it offers another viewpoint that validates the defensive patterns in this book.

The Healing

Healing is an important concept. Healing does not look like a constant state of peace and being unaffected by emotional situations—that is disconnection and dissociation. Healing looks like acceptance and being at peace with one's humanness. It means knowing what you are feeling, accepting what you are feeling with an understanding of where it comes from, and it looks like freedom to express your feelings in a way your body needs.

I joke with my clients that my work is to help them reconnect with their inner toddlers. Toddlers express their emotions but don't have a developed prefrontal cortex yet, so they cannot control when they express or put into words what they are feeling to be understood. We can do that, but we should not lose the ability to convey through the body when we develop that skill. Expression in words, cognitive understanding, and somatic freedom are keys to true healing.

Throughout the following chapters, I discuss "armoring patterns." These are defensive strategies and patterns that your mind and body utilize to protect you from life. These can be linked and understood through the diagnosis of Complex Post-Traumatic Stress Disorder and represent different armoring patterns related to this disorder. They are distinct from personality types in modern psychology because they involve psychological, physiological, and energetic armoring to define them. These patterns operate subconsciously, and very likely, you don't consciously realize how much they protect you. It is also extremely common for a pattern to be a mix of many or all of the defensive strategies, even if one is more dominant.

CHAPTER 4

ELUSIVE ARMOR

Without awareness of bodily feeling and attitude, a person becomes split into a disembodied spirit and a disenchanted body.
—Dr. Alexander Lowen

Elusive Armor is easy to run away in. It is light and it is camouflage, so you can be present but go unnoticed. Typically, children build Elusive Armor if trauma occurs from *in utero* to six months old. The armor is based on the developmental theme of this age, the time when they need to feel safe, depending fully on their caregiver. This armoring pattern is related to Lowen's first character structure, the Schizoid, and is best described by people like Anne, a slight 36-year-old woman with large eyes as if she were in a continual state of surprise.

When I first met Anne, I could sense her fear; she spent most of the time looking at the ground and only meeting my eyes when she connected with something I said. Her breath was so shallow I often didn't know if she was breathing. She usually wanted to stay at home and never leave. She described an eating disorder that caused her to be extremely thin; she felt that if she were smaller, others would not notice her. She was trying to disappear. Anne desired the love she read about in books and saw in movies, but felt she could only watch life pass from the sidelines. She expressed a deep desire to find a connection, but her behaviors do not allow for this possibility.

Anne was one who hid. She had trauma of existence. Anne wore Elusive Armor. In every situation, she felt unwanted and that her existence was not welcome. This armoring pattern can stem from the mother being consistently and sustainably stressed during pregnancy and possibly worried about the pregnancy. It can also result from pregnancy complications or birthing trauma. The mother may struggle to feel connected to the child in the early months. She may be withdrawn from the child or feel burdened or stressed over the child's needs. In some cases, the mother may feel hostile towards the infant.

During our first sessions, Anne would mentally "leave the room to find safety in the clouds." She would scream in fear, then switch to thinking about what she was going to have for lunch next Monday. She would process deep fear through breath work, and almost instantaneously, her eyes would gloss over, and she would say, "I just started to think about this book I was reading," or "Why do you think I'm so scared?" She wanted to talk about her emotions rather than feel them because talking is safer.

Over time, Anne shared that her mother became pregnant with her while planning to leave her father. Anne's father was abusive. Her mother felt overwhelmed after discovering she was pregnant; she endured his abuse throughout the pregnancy. Also, she knew she would have to endure that abuse for a longer time because she feared not being able to support her daughter.

Anne's mother attended one of our healing sessions and shared, "I loved her from the moment I met her, but my own fear wouldn't let me feel the love until I was out of the situation with her father." She said that after Anne was born, she once again began to plan her escape and was even more passionate because she knew Anne would one day be subjected to her father's rage. "At that time, keeping her safe was my way to show love. It wasn't holding Anne and nurturing her. I am learning she felt unloved because I couldn't love her in that way. But, damn, did I love her. My love just had to be in the form of war."

Through talk and bodywork, individually and with her mom, Anne began to heal. She found reasons to connect with people and began to feel fulfilled in relationships rather than drained. She began to feel less afraid. Anne began to feel more comfortable taking up space in the world around her.

Just as I saw with Anne, someone who wears this armor is typically slender, not wanting to take up much space. They tend to eat less because they feel deserving of less, unconsciously or consciously. Their large eyes appear frozen in a state of shock. In their presence, you may feel alone or anxious because it is difficult to connect with them, although they seemingly want to connect with you. It is not that they don't have needs; they just deem them as unimportant or rely on meeting all of their needs themselves. The crucial function of their protection is to keep someone else happy by not bothering anyone, so that the person they are attached to will not mind staying just connected enough with them to keep them alive.

Their main struggle is the fear that underlies most other struggles that are present. These individuals are almost always afraid of existing and struggle with many aspects of the external world, including vulnerability and connection. Clients with this armoring take as little as possible from life. During our first sessions, Ann would carefully grab one tissue and fold it in many directions until she had used every inch. It wasn't that she felt she didn't deserve a second tissue; it was that she didn't feel the right to exist in my office. For

Anne, her existence—her presence—was a burden to me. She began each connection she made in her life feeling unwanted.

Individuals wearing this armor hold many great qualities as well. They tend to be independent and self-sufficient, creative, rational, and introspective. They are often creators and innovators.

When Clara came to me, she had issues at work due to "freezing" and being unable to engage in tasks that she felt uncertain about. She was a part-time author and had written many books, but she had never submitted them for publication. She worked from home because being in the work environment with others was too stressful. Her boss was understanding and allowed her to work remotely. However, as work pressure built, she struggled and missed deadlines. She feared losing her job and that her boss "would hate her." Previously, Clara had been diagnosed with schizoaffective disorder. She presented with a meek voice and restricted affect. She did not make eye contact with me the entire first session, and in later sessions, when she made eye contact, it was both intense and absent.

We began with grounding work because whenever we discussed difficult topics, including her job performance, she would stop talking for a while and ask if she could write down what she was thinking instead. She had no voice. Once we started to ground, she experienced fear, so we moved and breathed slowly. After many grounding sessions, we began working on the fear. She had experienced early and likely unknown trauma, so we worked with particular bioenergetic exercises that explored early traumas. Upon processing, I realized that Clara was processing the trauma of her birth. She began to struggle to "get out." She felt "trapped" and that she was "going to die." After one session, Clara shared that she didn't have the memory but had begun to realize what she was processing.

"My mother told me that when I was born, she had gone into labor early. She had low amniotic fluid, and contractions began at 35 weeks. They tried to deliver me, but I got stuck in the birth canal. They used a plunger to try to remove me, but couldn't get me out. I nearly died. They rushed my mom to the operating room, where she underwent a cesarean. I was in the NICU for several weeks." Clara shared that her mom also struggled to connect because she was anxious about her health for much of her life.

I was amazed watching Clara piece together the story that her body had begun to tell us. Eventually, she processed the fear and landed in some intense sadness for her infant self, who came into this world feeling unwelcome because she had faced death before she was truly able to face life. This process led to immense healing for Clara and tremendous respect for this work. Eventually, she quit her job and began to publish her books. I am still tearful as I write Clara's story.

Physical Armoring

Elusive Armor must hold everything together, yet not take up too much space in the world. These individuals typically have thin and tense bodies, and they are in a constant state of bracing. Due to extensive tension in the diaphragm, their breath appears nonexistent; the breath remains primarily in the chest, and inhalation is quick. The individual will have extreme flexibility or inflexibility due to stiffness in the muscles. Like Clara, this individual's eyes are probably wide, and their facial muscles are tight. Individuals may experience difficulty in regulating their body temperature, and consequently, their feet are often cold. Sometimes, these individuals struggle with neck pain and migraines due to the extreme tension at the base of the skull.

Psychological Armoring

The Elusive Armor's narrative tends to be based on shame and deep fear. The fear is deeply rooted in shame because to be unlovable and therefore unlovable to your parents means you are unwanted, and this threatens your survival. Therefore, deep fear develops related to being wanted and lovable almost as a mechanism to survive. These individuals typically do not speak ill of others and often shoulder all blame in relationships. They believe they are the unlovable ones, and if anyone wrongs them, it is because of something they have done or who they are. The ones who don Elusive Armor have flights of ideas and are true dreamers. They may become invested in specific ideas and subjects and will get lost in them, which makes it difficult for them to connect with others. They feel unwelcome in most environments, so they tend to minimize the need for connection in their lives. They will describe themselves as introverts and present with a diagnosis associated with anxiety disorders.

> Common Psychological Armoring Patterns Associated with Elusive Armor
>
> 1. I am not worthy of connection.
> 2. I am safer when I am alone.
> 3. People will reject or abandon me.
> 4. I don't need others to survive.
> 5. I can't trust others to meet my needs.
> 6. I am not capable of true intimacy.
> 7. My emotions are too overwhelming for others.
> 8. Being vulnerable makes me weak.
> 9. I am different from others, and that makes me unlovable.

10. I have no right to ask for help or support.
11. It's better to keep my distance to avoid pain.
12. I must remain detached to protect myself.
13. I don't deserve the kind of love I seek.
14. Others will take advantage of me if I let them in.
15. I cannot rely on others, only on myself.

Energetic Armoring

Others often describe someone who wears Elusive Armor as "all over the place." Such a person speaks tangentially due to their flight of ideas, or they may not speak much at all. They live mostly "in their heads" and often are daydreaming, thinking up new ideas, or overanalyzing their lives. They tend to be energetic but create tension to avoid showing it. Imagine someone tightly holding onto a limb hovering over a cliff—that is this armor's energy. Their adrenaline is pumping, and they feel the energy pulsating through them, but they cannot move for fear of losing everything if they make one mistake. When looking into their eyes, you will make contact, but you may feel like no one is there at first.

Due to not being fully aware of their body, these individuals will often complain about being unable to connect with others or describe their emotions. This is not because they don't know what they feel, but because they don't know how to connect with others when they are feeling. They don't believe they have a right to exist, so they exist as minimally as possible. These individuals will often behave as if they have connections, but they never truly feel connected.

Relationship Armoring

Interestingly, individuals with specific armoring patterns frequently carry these same patterns into their relationships. The ones who wear Elusive Armor find themselves in relationships with highly emotional, expressive people who take up a lot of space. They find themselves with individuals who wear Need Armor or Control Armor. In early relationships, these individuals present as being engaged. However, as the relationship goes on, their connection remains superficial because they are too scared to connect, which causes their partners to believe that they are not caring and don't truly love.

These individuals tend to find themselves in arguments, and yet, they are confused about the reason for the arguments. They dissociate by donning their Elusive Armor at any sign of conflict or discontentment; they will stay in the room physically, but mentally, they have left. The partner often feels this distance and understands it as a lack of care, which is the furthest from the case. Consequently, their partners typically bring them to therapy because the individual wearing Elusive Armor "can't handle" their partner's emotions.

When doing couples therapy, the work will often be about teaching the elusive armor wearers to stay grounded in themselves during conflict while teaching their partners to slow down and give space. Frequently, this leads to both partners feeling more connected, which lessens the day-to-day problems. This process requires a lot of work on both sides and may include individual therapy. This process sounds logical and straightforward, but emotionally, it is a complex dynamic that can take years to improve sustainably. The individual needs to learn about themselves, their needs, and their boundaries, and to use this uniqueness to connect with others. Once the elusive armorer can stay grounded in all aspects of themselves during conflict, they will need to express their needs and learn to set boundaries to help them feel safe in connection with others.

The Enneagram Comparison

An individual wearing Elusive Armor would probably be an Enneagram Type 5 (the Investigator) or Type 6 (the Loyalist).

For a Five, the core motivation is fear of being overwhelmed by others and the world, leading to a desire for isolation and intellectual detachment. Someone who wears Elusive Armor or is a Five withdraws from emotional intimacy to protect themselves, and they may rely on intellectualization or retreat to manage emotional discomfort. The main difference I see between a Five and an individual wearing Elusive Armor is that the one in armor may be more physically withdrawn or shut off. In contrast, Fives are typically more concerned with accumulating knowledge and understanding.

Enneagram Type 6, often referred to as the Loyalist, is driven by a need for security and stability, which can manifest in a deep fear of uncertainty and a tendency to seek support from trusted authorities or systems. This can overlap with the elusive armoring pattern, which typically involves emotional detachment and withdrawal from others in order to protect oneself from perceived threats or overwhelm. Both types may struggle with trust and vulnerability. However, a Six's anxiety tends to manifest outwardly in seeking reassurance, while individuals wearing Elusive Armor tend to cope with fear by withdrawing and focusing on self-reliance. Despite these differences, both share an underlying desire to maintain safety and avoid emotional chaos.

The Healing

The first step of healing and putting down Elusive Armor begins with feeling safe and worthy of connection. Often, when bioenergetics is an appropriate intervention for the client, the client sits across from me with their eyes closed and breathes deeply into the belly. I ask them to connect with themselves before connecting with me. If they feel themselves mentally "leaving" or going somewhere else, such as thinking about what they will have for lunch or thinking about nothing, I encourage them to close their eyes and return to themselves. I teach them that being present and inside their bodies is their number one goal, even if that means not being able to connect with others in the ways requested. We work to find safety in connection through somatic work. We work together to empower the individual to express emotions related to the struggles with connection, and then normalize taking up space in connections. We do a lot of grounding and self-possession work. These individuals need to come home to their body and take ownership of who they are and their right to have a place in the world.

Following the connection and grounding work, we address multiple layers of healing. As individuals begin to repossess themselves, they experience a lot of fear, which they must process in layers. This healing may involve exercises to promote shaking, screaming, crying, and other forms of emotional expression to help the body release its tension or armor. The length of time for this work will vary, but individuals who practice grounding will experience some relief each time they ground. I encourage individuals to utilize these skills in their relationships to integrate the idea of self-possession with others in their lives.

Beliefs to Reach Through the Healing Journey

1. I am worthy of love, connection, and belonging.
2. It is safe for me to open my heart to others.
3. I trust that meaningful relationships enrich my life.
4. I can experience deep connections and still be myself.
5. I am capable of both giving and receiving love.
6. My emotions are valid, and it is safe for me to express them.
7. I am learning to trust others and let them meet my needs.
8. Vulnerability is a strength, not a weakness.
9. I deserve nurturing and care from others.
10. It is okay for me to need others and ask for help when I need it.
11. I am learning to integrate love and connection into my life.
12. I trust that opening up to others will bring me deeper healing.
13. It is safe to be seen for who I truly am.
14. I am open to new experiences of intimacy and closeness.
15. I can build relationships that nourish my soul and help me grow.

CHAPTER 5

NEED ARMOR

> *Sustenance for the infant and child is more than alimentary nourishment. The child needs love, security.*
>
> —Dr. Alexander Lowen

The next armoring pattern in the order in which the trauma is developed is Need Armor. This individual wears armor of selflessness and resentment to armor themselves against needing. Need armor typically begins to form if trauma occurs between 6 and 18 months of age. The trauma typically involves an issue within a person's ability to depend on the caregivers' nurturance.

I see this most often when the child's needs are too much for the caregiver, whether that is a child's sleep needs, their need to be fed, or their need to be held. Children's needs can be intense for parents, and they cannot communicate their needs. This can lead to the caregiver feeling frustrated with the child for having needs, and consequently, the child learns the pattern that they need too much, leading to shame. This armoring pattern also develops when the child's needs are consistently secondary to the parent's needs.

Some therapists and mentors argue that this trauma is present, to some degree, in all of us due to parents lacking the resources to fully care for their children. Parents are set up to fail. They don't have enough support, time, and stability to meet every need of their growing infant, who has a lot of needs. I have had clients in my office process somatic experiences of being left to cry in a crib when they were hungry or needing connection, feeling as though they might die. I've also had clients recall being toddlers, experiencing consistent frustration from a parent while they whined for something, unable to express their needs because they lacked the words. Again, I emphasize that not all children who experience these situations will develop the armoring pattern. To develop, these patterns require **chronic** exposure to such experiences.

This often brings up the topic of sleep training, particularly certain methods where children are left to cry in their cribs until they fall asleep. While this is an extremely complex subject that's beyond the scope of this book, I will say that not all babies who undergo sleep training experience it as trauma, and not all will develop this armoring pattern. However, some absolutely do, and I have worked with clients in my office who have processed this experience. Clients suffering from the more severe forms of this trauma experience increased distress. These clients either are combative from the beginning or cooperative, almost too cooperative.

However, they also have wonderful traits! Individuals wearing this armor tend to be compassionate, nurturing, affectionate, generous, and they are great listeners. They tend to live in extremes and often present to me with a diagnosis of Bipolar Disorder or Borderline Personality Disorder, but can also present with depressive and anxiety disorders.

The Body's Armor

One of the first things to notice about individuals with this armoring is their arms, which appear lifeless, as if they are not part of the body; their hands are cold. This powerful clue has to do with the person's adaptation of needing something or not reaching out. Then, notice the collapse of the chest. These individuals often hunch over, as if they have been kicked in the stomach and folded forward. Their breathing is shallow; almost no movement occurs in the chest. The feet of these individuals may turn in; their legs may appear strong, but they have limited connection or grounding. These individuals typically have a lot of tension in their neck and face. Many struggle with migraines.

The Psychological Armoring

The narrative of someone who wears Need Armor is that others cannot and will not meet their needs. They begin to believe they don't need much but often begin to ask for a lot or become angry when their needs aren't met in relationships, even if they are not communicating those needs. The clients who present with the defensive pattern of Need Armor present in two ways. Sometimes, they are cooperative and engaged in therapy; they are the "best clients," requesting resources, homework, and anything that can help them. Over time, you realize nothing you provide is enough. You can give the client every magical resource known to man, and they will still not "get better" because they are not genuinely seeking to be "healed." This is the most common manifestation I see. They are diagnosed with Borderline Personality Disorder and sent to my office.

The second extreme is the client who is immediately disheartened and depressed. They don't believe anything will work and live in a state of passive helplessness. They think you are the only one who can help them, and they initially state that they are not willing to help themselves. Often, they participate in self-harming behavior and don't see a way of stopping, as it is the only comfort they know. They show up session after session but don't engage much and report not getting much out of the sessions.

For all patterns of this armoring, clients are often more focused on making the therapist or others in relationships happy than themselves. They tend to present as people pleasers with a deep desire and focus on the comfort of those around them. They are fearful of having needs and needs not being met. Both therapists and clients may leave the sessions feeling confused and defeated. A colleague once shared about a client with this armoring pattern: "It's like they show up to the session just to punish me! I try so hard, and nothing seems like enough."

The reality is they do not mean to punish, although they may act in a punishing way. They don't know what or how they need, so they allow themselves to express only what they think they are allowed to need, which leads to feelings of frustration for them and often those trying to help them. Due to this, I have found much of the early work to be encouraging and validating the expression of their needs, setting healthy and consistent boundaries to allow predictability of their ability to meet needs, and allowing them to process disappointment when needs are not able to be met.

Common Psychological Armoring Patterns Associated with Need Armor

1. I am not enough on my own.
2. I am dependent on others to feel good about myself.
3. I must constantly seek approval or care from others.
4. I am not worthy of receiving love without giving something in return.

5. My needs will never be fully met.
6. If I stop giving, I will be abandoned.
7. I must please others to avoid rejection.
8. I feel empty and incomplete without others' attention or affection.
9. I am powerless without others to care for me.
10. I am afraid of being left alone with my feelings.

The Energetic Armoring

Individuals with this armoring appear to have a lot of energy, but it is not true energy; it is manufactured by anxiety or some "upper" like caffeine or stimulants. The first clue may be short bursts of energy followed by periods of depression. These energy bursts are due to low energy, and the individuals often "power up" to appear energetic and alive. Individuals with this adaptation tend to have a wide range of feelings and express them with emotion, but underneath their expression is tremendous pressure and anxiety due to their fear of not being understood or being "too much."

Often, it feels as if these individuals speak one hundred miles an hour, but they never truly connect with what their emotions require. They treat therapy like a drop-and-go situation; they come to sessions to drop something, then feel somewhat better, only to need to do the same thing the following week. They never truly receive what they need because they are afraid to. This often leads to hopelessness, emptiness, and disappointment within them. They are afraid to get what they need to heal, which creates an extreme push-and-pull relationship within the therapeutic dynamic.

Relationship Armoring

For someone wearing Need Armor, relationships are probably one of the most complicated aspects of their lives. They tend to develop relationships with partners who are calm, stoic, emotionally shut down, and don't require much emotional space on the surface. This partner can either be wearing Elusive Armor, Control Armor, or Endurance Armor. They typically begin the relationship presenting few needs and being the "cool and laid back partner." As they become more comfortable, they present with extreme needs that the partner cannot meet.

Beth and Joey were a younger couple who met in college.

"Beth used to love to go to football games with me and my friend. She would drink my friends under the table and was the life of the party. I don't know what happened."

When Joey shared this type of rhetoric in our couples sessions, I saw Beth brace herself by clenching her jaw and raising her shoulders. She would fight back.

"Your friends are bad people. I started to realize they are bad people, and I'm not safe with them. Football is not safe; it is a barbaric sport, and I just started to realize that!"

The issue was likely not Joey's friends or football suddenly becoming unsafe. The issue was that as Beth grew closer to Joey, she began to feel more unsafe. Someone wearing Need Armor longs to feel safe and loved in relationships, but due to how they view themselves, which is often extremely negative and shame-based, when someone gets close, they start to fear that their partner will "see them" and their needs and run! So, they create a sense of "safety" by trying to isolate themselves, ideally with their partner, where they feel safest. They have a scarcity mindset, meaning they feel the resources around them, such as attention and love, are scarce. Therefore, they need to be their partner's only focus to increase the likelihood of their needs being met.

This is not a conscious action, but one linked to the development stage of their trauma.

For those of you who are parents, think back to the toddler years; it is not uncommon for young children to want to be alone with their caretaker. I remember going to dinner with a friend and my two-year-old son, and he would go from my sweet, cooperative son to a grumpy and demanding toddler, all because he didn't want to share my attention. It was hard to share my attention with my friend. When attention is or has been a scarce resource, sharing it can feel threatening. We can apply this concept to Beth and Joey.

Over time, it became evident that Beth felt shame and disconnected from Joey. At first, she suggested that Joey go to the football games with his friends while she stayed home. However, before every football game, Beth and Joey would begin to argue. Sometimes, they argued about how Joey acted before the game or if he didn't tell her when he was leaving. Other times, it would be about something completely unrelated. They would fight, and Joey would often say he would stay home. Then, Beth would tell him that she would feel "too bad" if he didn't go, so she had to go too. If he did go, they would have a worse argument when he returned, or they would fight through text messages during the game. It was immensely confusing for Joey and Beth, but not for me.

When Beth first started couples and individual therapy, she felt defeated and defensive. She believed her black-and-white thinking and asked questions that made me question myself: "Are you saying that two men hitting each other as hard as they can isn't barbaric?" Although I couldn't agree or disagree, I enjoyed her arguments and processed them with her, not agreeing or disagreeing with her logic, but always trying to help her identify and express her underlying feelings and needs related to the issues. I emphasized how she felt in her body and what she needed, rather than what she thought and believed everyone else should also think.

Individuals with Need Armor will often argue to have others view things the way they do because this may reduce their shame related to their own individual feelings and needs. This stems from the adaptive strategy that if we all think and feel the same way, then there is no shame in it.

I continually brought Beth back to her struggle to feel safe in relationships, and through individual sessions, we gradually began to explore bodywork. We did exercises focusing on the shame of having needs, as this is the underlying trauma of this armoring pattern. Over time, Beth's combativeness gave way to immense sadness. She mourned not being good enough or lovable enough for someone to want to take care of her and meet her needs. Her grief began with her believing that Joey did not want to do this; on the contrary, he was willing, but not to the extreme of losing himself and his identity. Eventually, Beth's grief led us to her true story.

Beth was the youngest of six children. Her parents had limited resources. Beth's mother stayed at home for the other children but returned to work when Beth was born. She no longer wanted to be home with the children, and her older siblings were old enough to look after her. She remembered being alone a lot and wondering where her mom was. Beth believed her mom was happy to see her siblings when she came home from work, but not her, because she would cry and want to be held. Beth wanted to enter her parents' bedroom at night and sleep next to her mother to feel the closeness she longed for all day, but her mother would put her back into her room, often in anger. Beth had memories of crying in hunger some nights, and no one coming to feed her. She felt fear in her body as she processed these memories.

As Beth grew older, her family members recognized her as needy, which led Beth to believe this about herself. Rather than believe she received too little, she believed she needed too much. So, she began to try not to need anything from anyone; however, this is not sustainable.

As relationships grow, needs grow. As an adult, Beth began to battle her partners externally when, in reality, she was battling herself. She was battling the part of her that needs against the part of her that hates herself for needing. No partner she came in contact with could win this fight because Beth was playing a losing game.

If we deny our needs and feel ashamed of them, we can't simply ask for a need to be met and wait for an answer. Much like emotions, if needs are repressed, they will only become stronger and be expressed in dysregulation. If we can't set boundaries, we adopt a passive-aggressive manner to get our needs met. In some cases, individuals with this armoring pattern are described as "manipulative" because their shame prevents them from directly asking for what they need; they set themselves up to fail by asking for what they need in a way that is often threatening or so passive that others don't understand.

I have had many clients with this armoring pattern contemplate suicide because of how hopeless they feel in their lives. They are desperate to get their needs met, but feel it is impossible to do so. People in their lives often describe feeling as if "nothing they do is good enough." In reality, the clients' real needs aren't being met, and therefore, nothing satiates their needs.

> **If we can't set boundaries, we adopt a passive-aggressive manner to get our needs met.**

Individuals with this defensive pattern may ask you to stay with them instead of leaving on a trip, or they may ask you to reach out to them 15 times a day. To test your loyalty, they may promote arguments and tell you to leave because they don't want to be in connection with you anymore. However, their basic need is to know they are important, they matter, and therefore they are safe. They are desperately searching for a secure attachment and safety.

To reduce the intensity of the need for certainty within their attachments, the individual must process the original wounding. They must process their original feeling of abandonment, not to fear being abandoned as intensely. Current relationships can reenact the trauma and may help heal the wounds slowly over time, but few relationships in this dynamic have the stamina to continue without some understanding from the individual with the defense pattern and their ability to work through their underlying trauma.

The Enneagram Comparison

Need Armor wearers are most like the Enneagram Type 2 (the Helper).

The Two's core motivation is the fear of being unloved or feeling unimportant, leading to a strong desire to be needed and valued by others. Someone wearing Need Armor and a Two seeks emotional support and reassurance from others, often over-extending themselves to fulfill others' needs to gain love and acceptance. They value the opinions of others more than their own.

While the individual wearing Need Armor may have a general feeling of emptiness or insecurity, Twos are more likely to focus on being helpful and nurturing to fill this gap.

The Healing

The healing process for someone wearing Need Armor focuses on addressing the individual's deep-seated emotional needs related to dependency, nourishment, and trust. People with this armor often exhibit behaviors linked to a fear of abandonment or deprivation, manifesting as excessive neediness, difficulties with boundaries, or overindulgence (e.g., overeating, smoking, or excessive talking). These individuals often have tightness or tension in the throat, jaw, and chest, which can symbolize emotional restrictions related to expressing needs, desires, and feelings.

Healing begins with helping the person reconnect with their body and become more aware of these physical tensions, using techniques like deep breathing and body awareness to release them. The therapist encourages the individual to explore their early experiences of nourishment and attachment, as issues from infancy and early childhood, such as neglect or inconsistent caregiving, often underpin this defensive pattern. We work on expressing needs physically through reaching out in a variety of ways.

By acknowledging and processing feelings of deprivation, insecurity, and unmet needs, the individual can start to develop healthier emotional responses. Additionally, strengthening self-acceptance and fostering a sense of safety and trust is crucial in this healing process. Bioenergetic exercises help individuals gradually build confidence in their ability to self-soothe and meet their own needs, reducing the compulsion to seek constant external validation or security. As the person learns to assert their own boundaries, express their needs directly, and trust themselves, they can move toward greater emotional independence and more balanced relationships.

Beliefs to Be Reached Through the Healing Journey

1. I am whole and complete as I am.
2. I am deserving of love and care, without needing to earn it.
3. It is safe for me to rely on myself and meet my own needs.
4. I trust that I can find fulfillment from within.
5. I am worthy of receiving love freely and without conditions.
6. I am not afraid of being alone; I am enough on my own.
7. I am learning to trust myself and my own inner resources.
8. I do not need to seek approval to feel valued.
9. I can give and receive love freely, without fear of loss.
10. It is okay to express my needs and desires without fear of rejection.

CHAPTER 6

ENDURANCE ARMOR

> *Unfortunately, most people do not stop to feel their tiredness. Faced with the pressures of life, they believe that it is a matter of survival to go on as they have been. Feeling tired raises a deep fear that they may not be able to continue the struggle. Many find it difficult to say, "I can't." As children, they were taught that where there's a will, there's a way. To say, "I can't," is to admit failure, which is seen as evidence that they are unworthy of love.*
> —Dr. Alexander Lowen

Individuals who keep on going no matter what crumble under the weight of their armor, but their endurance has kept them alive. These people have an interesting blend of persistence and helplessness. This armor begins to form if a child faces trauma from the ages of 18 months to 4 years old. The trauma typically involves being neglected, criticized, or emotionally deprived as they begin to demonstrate their will. Their shame circles around feelings of worthlessness and a belief that they deserve hardship and pain.

It is a normal developmental stage for toddlers to begin exerting their will and their control. They go from being a part of the mother where there is no distinguishable separation between the two of them to wanting to be themselves *and* loved by their mother and other caregivers. If caregivers are consistently critical, abusive or shame the child as they begin to become themselves, this action leads to them believing that they have no worth.

Endurance armored people likely went through control battles with their parents; even if the child was passive during these battles, the parents wanted the child to know they held the control. This is known as *power over* in the therapist world. Power over is the concept that one with more resources can control the actions of someone else. It is not a collaborative process and involves shame and fear to control the "lesser beings." People who utilize power over control do not exhibit empathy, understanding, or compromise, leading to a battle of the wills in which someone must break, and it is typically the child. It is common for someone to put on Endurance Armor following physical and sexual abuse because the child feels no control over their body, needs, and decisions. Endurance Armor can also be donned when the child is consistently criticized, rejected, or shamed for just being themselves. This means having their own emotions, thoughts, and needs.

Those wearing Endurance Armor often gain control by making sure others know they are unhappy in their lives. This gives them some control because, although they may not be able to choose how they live, they can control whether or not they like it. Most things feel like an obligation to someone wearing this armor, even things they previously enjoyed. Eventually, things they may genuinely like to enjoy become tainted with this negative energy, turning everything negative. They may also try to passively control situations because they believe outward expression of needs or feelings will only be met with criticism. An example: instead of telling someone how they hurt them, they may withdraw from the relationship in order to either punish the individual who hurt them and/or protect themselves. They are also extremely resilient, self-sacrificing, altruistic, attuned to another's pain, and dutiful.

Anthony presented to me with depression. He was unmarried and had few romantic relationships. He had close friends but struggled to feel safe with them. He felt that, at any moment, he might make a mistake, his friends would abandon him, and he would be alone. He was terrified of this happening and already felt incredibly lonely.

He had a stocky build and rarely made eye contact. He appeared to have low energy but described building a successful business career. He owns his home, is at the top tier of the law firm he works for, and is fiercely independent.

When I first met Anthony, I knew something didn't add up. How could someone so fearless in their career be so fearful in their connections? As I sat with him, I realized he is a trauma soldier clad in Endurance Armor. Anthony described enduring all sorts of things for his friends but never requested anything in return. He described putting himself through a rigorous school program with no help from family. He would exclaim, "I don't need anyone!" I remember frequently asking Anthony, "Why then are you here?"

"I don't need anyone. I may want to know what it is like to be loved, though," Anthony brilliantly assured me.

Anthony's story came to life through talk therapy and, later, bodywork. His mother died when he was extremely young. His father began to drink and became abusive to Anthony and his younger siblings. He started to learn exactly how to act around his father to keep him calm. He would protect his siblings by keeping things as calm as possible by doing everything he knew to do to keep his father happy. Eventually, his father remarried and sent him away to live with his grandparents.

When Anthony was young, he remembered fearing his new family would send him to foster care if he acted up due to a previous threat made by his grandmother when Anthony wouldn't listen to her. Anthony's grandmother had many opinions about how he should act. She didn't like him exerting any control or will. If he did, she would withdraw from him completely or send him to his room with vague threats of sending him away. Anthony lived in fear until he was 16; that's when he left for college early due to his outstanding academic performance. Through processing, Anthony began to get in touch with extreme rage and protest, which he was not allowed to have as a child. Later, he began to process profound fear related to him being unable to trust his security.

"My mom is DEAD! She left me with an abusive father! Then, my father sent me away. Wasn't I good enough for them? Then, my grandparents are burdened with me, and I can be cut out at any minute."

Imagine this child's fear of authority and why their will would be broken. Whenever they expressed their will, it was met with physical and verbal abuse and threats of abandonment. This taught Anthony that he can only trust himself and must create an environment in which he can be safe, an environment he builds and secures. Only he is responsible for his safety. Resentment for life and disdain for responsibility build, but this is the only option to survive.

This is the common theme, although not a common story, of the ones who wear Endurance Armor. These individuals frequently have an involved parent or caregiver who has power over control.

Rachel is another common example of this character pattern. She was a 22-year-old female brought to me by her parents for her failure to launch. Her parents felt frustrated, feeling they had no way to motivate Rachel anymore, and they were right. Rachel was at a standstill. She was depressed and disheartened. She felt like a loser and believed she could not do anything.

Through talk therapy and bodywork, Rachel and I discovered that her will was broken. Her parents, especially her mother, had told her what to do and how to do it from day one. If Rachel stepped out of the parameters set by her mother, her mother would become angry and punish Rachel by yelling at her, then disconnecting for several days. Her father ignored the dynamic and never stood up for Rachel. When she turned 18, she began to feel lost and depressed. She wasn't happy with the path her parents had put her on, but believed that she couldn't do anything without them, so she began to stand still. Moving Rachel took years; it took lots of anger release and empowerment to reunite Rachel's natural protest for herself and her life. She is now a therapist in her own practice.

The Body's Armor

Most individuals who carry this armor are stocky; they look strong as an ox, as if they could hold up the world. Their neck tends to be short, and their pelvis pulled forward. These individuals are not very flexible and do not move gracefully, although they move with purpose. The breathing pattern appears normal until some pressure is applied, and they begin to tighten up to "batten down the hatches" to endure this next war, which leads to holding their breath in and restricting it. Their body appears defeated in relaxation, yet they hold a lot of tension in the shoulders, back, neck, chest, and abdomen. The leg muscles are often well-defined and tense to hold the person up when the individual desires to collapse in exhaustion.

The Psychological Armoring

Individuals who wear Endurance Armor most often present with a diagnosis related to depressive symptoms, such as major depressive disorder, treatment-resistant depression, dysthymia, bipolar disorder, and cyclothymic disorders. They often carry the narrative that life is hard, relationships are hard, and everything is too hard. Getting out of bed is often difficult for these individuals, but they don't give themselves any breaks. They want to engage in life because they want to, not because they have to, but they don't know how. These individuals carry passive helplessness narratives and feel powerless over their life or existence. Even if they appear extremely powerful and successful, they may feel powerless over being able to rest. Often, they tend to feel stuck.

Also, they can be extremely overly functional and not admit to themselves that anything is complicated! Individuals with this armor tend to be very successful or unsuccessful, depending primarily on whether they express their anger inwardly or outwardly. However, the individual is angry with either of these expressive tendencies.

If the client presents with anger with themselves and believes everyone else is good, then they likely are limited in their lives because they believe they are incapable. If they are more angry externally, they will likely be more action-oriented to fight against something. They are soldiering either for or against themselves. In either case, in an indirect way, they are protesting.

Common Psychological Armoring Patterns Associated with Endurance Armor

1. I must suffer to prove my worth.
2. My needs are not important; others' needs come first.
3. I am unworthy of joy and pleasure.
4. I am only loved if I endure hardship or pain.
5. I must sacrifice my happiness for others.

6. I deserve punishment for my mistakes or weaknesses.
7. I can't set boundaries without feeling guilty.
8. I am not allowed to prioritize my own needs.
9. I am weak if I ask for help or support.
10. I must endure hardship to be valued.

The Energetic Armoring

I describe their energy as similar to that of a burro. Burros can't be forced to do anything. If you try to force them to follow you, they dig their hooves into the ground and will not move, no matter how hard you pull. You have to build a relationship with them to help them feel safe enough to move forward. They must feel you accept them as they are before they will truly connect or engage. These individuals are tired, and their energy is depleted, but they typically keep functioning because they have to. They resent much of their life because it feels like an obligation rather than a choice. You can feel this underlying disdain for life in their energy, which leads to a feeling of negativity surrounding most, if not all, aspects of their lives. They often have a secret defiance that they will not express outwardly but you can feel it as you sit with them.

Relationship Armoring

These individuals will approach forming a relationship by being submissive or defiant. Over time, both defiance and submission play a role in their close relationships. Interestingly, I frequently see this armoring pattern in unattached persons who are not in a romantic relationship. They have had romantic relationships but, at some point, tend to feel invaded and become defiant to the closeness as the relationship develops. They tend to be in short-lived relationships with someone wearing Need Armor or Perfectionist Armor and, sometimes, in relationships with individuals wearing Control Armor. Often, the one who was raised to be a soldier begins the dynamic by being "tough to get" or being very submissive and "attached" up front, but pulling back as soon as the individual's partner applies any pressure for a relationship. They tend not to compromise much in relationships or compromise a lot, but with a lot of silent resentment that presents in some covert way.

Candace and Melissa demonstrated this dynamic. They were a couple on the brink of divorce. Melissa shared that even though she had been with Candace for 18 years, she didn't know her. She shared that she often felt that Candace was angry during an argument, but Candace wouldn't tell her what she was angry about. She shared that Candace was not happy with anything and felt that nothing she did could make her happy. The couple reported that, once in a while, Candace would get drunk and express a lot of dissatisfaction with the relationship, but would not continue the conversation when she was sober the next day. Candace would then go through a guilt spiral of how she needs to "get better" and stop hurting her wife, and she would sober up and soldier on. They came to me as a last-ditch effort to break this cyclic behavior. I began to work with each person individually before we met as a couple, which I felt was needed due to the immense difficulty in the dynamic.

When I first heard Candace's story, I wondered what repressed aggression surfaces when she is under the influence. I learned that Candace's father was highly domineering. He told her how to dress, what to eat, what to think, and who to be. He would berate Candace and even physically harm her if she did something he disagreed with. Her mother was a docile woman who never stepped in; Candace watched her father treat her mother the same way. If either of them pushed back, her father would become sad and state that his family is his life and that he does everything for them because he wants them to be safe. Candace felt sad for her father and guilty for speaking up because it hurt him. She learned it was easiest to comply. Candace donned Endurance Armor.

These sessions were long and hard, and the dynamics took years to sort out. We would get close; then Candace would get angry at me and stop therapy for a while or show up to sessions but talk less rather than sharing her anger directly with me. She felt that I was becoming her father and criticizing her for doing something wrong if I directly addressed a maladaptive behavior, but couldn't share this, so she would just leave or stonewall. Our sessions were a delicate dance, ensuring that Candace felt my care for her, while reinforcing her belief that I could stand on my own emotionally and would accept her as she expressed her truth, even if that meant she was angry at me. I could handle her anger.

Candace's wife, Melissa, was the head of a small, successful company when they met. She was extremely innovative, capable, and successful. Candace liked that she was independent and didn't need her. However, during the 10 years they had been together, Melissa had become a stay-at-home mom, and at Candace's recommendation, she began to do less and less. Candace began to do more and more. Melissa began to struggle with self-esteem and began to feel useless and vulnerable. I worked with Melissa on her right to exist as herself and to find worth in herself just for existing. At first, Candace had no complaints in her marriage, although she seemed withdrawn and unengaged. However, through individual work, Candace began to complain that Melissa was physically and emotionally unpredictable. She shared that she often feels criticized by Melissa and that if she doesn't provide everything for her, Melissa will become irate.

After a time, I began to see Melissa and Candace together to discuss the dynamics and see if we could do some couples bioenergetic work. Melissa processed feeling useless and guilty. She also discussed how she feels she can't do anything right. She shared that she feels Candace resents her for being useless and doesn't really care for her. These feelings likely contributed to Melissa's dysregulated behavior. Candace would appear depressed when Melissa shared this and expressed feelings. Candace would eventually feel guilty, believing she had made Melissa feel this way. When Candace would share her frustrations, Melissa would get triggered, believing Candace didn't really love her, and put on her Need Armor. Candace would then feel punished for sharing and like nothing she does is enough, reinforcing that she is worthless no matter how hard she tries, and it is unsafe to share her truth. Both partners couldn't allow their partner to feel emotion without being triggered to apply their armor. Their emotions became a threatening part of the relationship rather than the foundation of the relationship.

Melissa's Need Armor caused her to feel shame, believing she was not doing enough and relying too much financially on Candace. This caused her to be hypervigilant to Candace's feelings and look for signs that Candace was angry. Candace carried a lot of resentment and anger behind her armor from childhood, and Melissa could feel it. This felt extremely threatening to Melissa because she believed she had finally found someone with some desire to meet her needs, and she was terrified of losing that. As Melissa expressed her fear, the more Candace strapped to her back to prove her love, and the more silent resentment Candace built. This led to more episodes in which she would drink and "blow up." Whenever we would get to the last part of the dynamic, Candace would say, "There is no use in asking for more from Melissa, Kelly. She just can't handle it. I can, so even if it makes me miserable, I will keep doing what I have to do."

We had to find a way for Candace to speak her truth without triggering Melissa's Need Armor. We had to create a space and dynamic where both partners' needs could be met, and they could both have emotion without that becoming a threat to the other.

Over the years, the most powerful words Candace learned were "I can't." It became clear that instead of silently judging how Melissa couldn't do things, she needed to start telling Melissa, "I can't do this." For someone wearing Endurance Armor, this means laying down the armor and waving the white flag of vulnerability. By Candace doing this, Melissa could choose to approach Candace in vulnerability for both of them and begin to pick up what Candace couldn't carry. It was beautiful. If Melissa couldn't pick it up, the couple would discuss how to do it together. Both began to allow themselves and each other to have an identity and needs within the relationship.

Eventually, we reached the end of their therapy journey, and the couple is now one of the closest I have seen. I remember joking with Candace and Melissa as they left their last session: "Now, don't mess this up," I said, winking. Candace looked at me and said, "I can't," as she squeezed Melissa's hand. I will never forget that moment.

Enneagram Comparison

Endurance Armor is most similar to the Enneagram Type 9 (the Peacemaker).

Nines' core motivation is a fear of conflict and disconnection; thus, they seek harmony and peace, often by deferring to others and minimizing their own needs. Both someone wearing Endurance Armor and Nines may suppress their own desires and needs in favor of maintaining peace or avoiding discomfort, often yielding to others' wishes to keep the peace.

While Nines tend to suppress conflict and merge with others to avoid confrontation, the ones wearing Endurance Armor internalize their frustration and martyr themselves in response to their perceived inability to meet others' expectations.

The Healing

Healing for someone wearing Endurance Armor involves addressing the core emotional and physical patterns that underlie their behavior. The first step is to address their deep sense of unworthiness, tendency to suppress emotions, and pattern of self-sacrifice or self-punishment. Endurance Armor manifests as a rigid, defensive body posture, often marked by tightness in the chest, throat, and diaphragm, reflecting the emotional suppression and fear of fully experiencing vulnerability.

Somatic focuses on helping the individual reconnect with their body, release repressed emotions through expression of anger and sadness, and challenge the self-limiting beliefs that fuel their armor. This process often involves deep breathing exercises, physical movements, and postural changes, aimed at loosening muscular tension and allowing the individuals to release suppressed feelings, as well as expressive exercises. Through this somatic work, the individual can begin to experience emotions in a more authentic way, letting go of the inner conflict that manifests as self-punishment or martyrdom.

Emotional expression encourages the individual to develop healthier boundaries and self-compassion. As the individual learns to accept their own needs and desires without guilt or fear of rejection, they can shift from a self-sacrificial mindset to one that values their own well-being. Eventually, this process fosters a sense of self-worth and self-respect, enabling the individual to move away from patterns of self-inflicted suffering and towards a more balanced and empowered way of being.

> Beliefs to Be Reached Through the Healing Journey
>
> 1. I am worthy of love, care, and happiness without needing to suffer.
> 2. I have the right to prioritize my own needs and desires.
> 3. I am deserving of peace, joy, and pleasure in my life.
> 4. It is safe for me to receive help and support without guilt.
> 5. I release the belief that I must suffer to be loved.
> 6. I am learning to set healthy boundaries with love and respect.
> 7. I honor myself by valuing my own well-being.
> 8. I am not weak for expressing my needs or seeking care.
> 9. It is okay to say 'no' when it is best for me.
> 10. I am worthy of kindness, and I allow myself to receive it.

CHAPTER 7

CONTROL ARMOR

Because we are afraid of life, we seek to control or master it.
—Dr. Alexander Lowen

Control Armor is a deeply fastened and sturdy armor made of control. The need for control presents physically, psychologically, and emotionally through this armoring pattern. Control Armor begins to develop between 18 months and 4 years old. Control is often a comforting thought for any of us who struggle with the vulnerability that naturally exists in life. The reality is that we have command over very little. We can work hard our whole lives and still be harmed by life, other people, and even those closest to us. This reality is more difficult for someone with Control Armor to withstand.

In Lowen's character structures, this would be known as the Psychopath. Others have called this a narcissistic pattern; in our Western culture, we may label someone presenting with this armoring pattern with a personality disorder such as Narcissistic Personality Disorder. In today's society, a narcissist lacks empathy and manipulates and hurts others. These functions of the armoring pattern can definitely be present. Similar to the other armoring patterns, how these individuals wear their armor may negatively impact those around them. However, these individuals need not be shamed; they carry enough shame of their own. It is important to remember that just like all of the armoring patterns, these traits and behaviors are armor the individual wears, not who they are.

Due to how we view this armoring pattern when we interact with it, we do not offer understanding for these individuals. Individuals label their ex-partners, parents, and friends as "narcissists" with anger and resentment due to being hurt by them, which is completely understandable. This armoring pattern can absolutely cause harm to those who love the person under the armor. I am not here to say this shouldn't be felt; that would be against the whole premise of this book. I am here to educate you on what someone wearing Control Armor is likely going through and to challenge you to understand that almost all of us (if I am being brave, I will say all of us) have at least some of these traits at times. Many of us, when living in our armor, have some component of needing control of our surroundings to protect ourselves. To feel safe, we need to feel superior to others when having conflict or disagreement. The individuals wearing the thick armoring associated with this pattern behave this way much more frequently.

There is a spectrum of armoring patterns, and some wear their armor thinner than others. I have met individuals with this armoring pattern who aren't disconnected entirely from their empathy but are from their emotions.

Someone wearing Control Armor typically denies their feelings to control the perception of themselves or others. They may admit to feelings if it serves their image, but they rarely express them due to their need for control. This person does not lack empathy but admittedly denies it to the extent that they don't even

Many of us, when living in our armor, have some component of needing control of our surroundings to protect ourselves. To feel safe, we need to feel superior to others when having conflict or disagreement.

acknowledge it within themselves. The truth is that they have less empathy for themselves than all the other character defenses.

This character defense develops when a child is taken advantage of, humiliated, or used, typically by their primary caretakers or parents. It can also occur when a child is emotionally neglected by parents not setting boundaries or "spoiling them" with things but not emotionally connecting with them. A feeling of chronic rejection is the main ingredient associated with this armoring pattern. Examples include parents being overly excited when their child does well and excessively critical when their child doesn't. The child learns to turn against their humanness and perform over feel.

Parents who use their children against each other, whether in a divorce or to suit their own emotional needs, teach the child that the parent controls how the child feels. This leads the child to separate from their feelings; they learn how they are "supposed to feel" or how they are "supposed to think." We note more severe cases of this armoring pattern when a child experiences violence or witnesses violence within their family structure. I believe this comes from separating from the feelings they are experiencing due to struggling with what to feel. Do they love their parent, who is also their abuser, or do they hate them?

Both are true, but this is too much for the children to process, so they shut off their emotions. They begin to separate from their emotions, believing they can't trust them. In most cases, someone wearing this armor was more unsafe if they had empathy for the person harming them, usually a caregiver, so they separated from empathy. I have noticed this wounding can also occur in social settings outside the home, but the severity of the armoring pattern in this case tends to be less.

Children who grow up in environments where it is unsafe to have empathy typically develop some of this pattern of defensiveness. The degree to which this is true will merit the intensity of the defense, much like the other defensive patterns. If it is unsafe for you to have empathy, then it is safer for you to develop these traits. It isn't a character defect but rather a defense that ends painfully in the short and long terms.

Sarah came to me due to struggling in her marriage. She shared that she and her husband hadn't lived in the same home or had sexual intimacy in years, and she was tired of the situation. She talked a lot about what her husband had done and how he behaved. She shared a false and intellectual facade of empathy and understanding for her husband's upbringing through a cognitive and projected understanding of why her husband behaved this way. Sarah shared how something he had done impacted her, but then would justify and argue her husband's side. It was as if she were trying a court case in her mind that sounded condescending at times and fair at other times, but the verdict was already guilty.

She showed little emotion other than a fixed smile on her face. Sarah used theory and logic to evade my questions about emotions and feelings. Sometimes, I felt my head spinning, although it was Sarah's head that was spinning. She was ungrounded, separated from herself, and constantly trying to appear in control, well-adjusted, capable, and strong—everything her parents wanted her to be. In time, she shared her story.

Sarah's father sexually abused her from a very young age. She was unsure whether her mother knew about the abuse, but she felt she did. She said that her mom would comment that it was Sarah's job to keep her dad happy; those comments would make my skin crawl for Sarah, but Sarah appeared to feel nothing. She shared her family's intergenerational trauma when she shared her own trauma with me as if to justify what had happened to her intellectually. Sarah was not allowed to have any boundaries growing up. When she verbalized anger to her father, he would buy her and her mother something expensive. She would see the joy on her mom's face and be silent again. Sarah recounted feeling in complete control over whether her family unit was happy or not. She felt safe in this and initially ignored the immense burden of shame she carried because her family was never really happy.

For years, I saw Sarah. She controlled the sessions for quite a while, and I allowed this to help her feel safe. I was not going to compete for control. She would come in and vent about her husband, brother, and parents and psychoanalyze them all, but she never looked inwards. Her only form of protest was rationalization.

One day, after our relationship was strong, I tested Sarah. Before she arrived, I put out the bioenergetic cube and bat, a device to release anger. Sarah walked in, looked at it, and sat down. She asked me what it was, and I said, "I think we should release some of the anger in your body today. The anger that has frozen your face, neck, and shoulders."

Sarah paused.

It was the longest silence we had ever experienced in a session. Eventually, she took a breath, looked away from me, and spoke.

"I feel like when you are in one of those rides that drops you from high up in the air. I am nauseous."

"What do you think that feeling is, Sarah?" I replied, giving the power control back to her.

"I don't know, but I have had issues with migraines and headaches my whole life. That is the real reason I came to you. I feel so much tension at the base of my head."

Now, Sarah was different. These situations do not always go this well. I have had clients walk out, shame the methods, or simply ignore the object in the room. Sarah was ready for someone to invite her to do things differently. The next few sessions were about getting Sarah into her body, grounding, and having her approach the feeling of terror in her stomach. This led to a lot of emotional processing, beginning with rage, then moving to sadness and fear. Sarah frequently threw bioenergetic tantrums and went over to the bioenergetic breathing stool. She began to demonstrate empathy for others and, as I write this book, is still working on developing more empathy for herself. After about 10 bioenergetic sessions, we never discussed her marriage again because she felt she was unable to be intimate due to her inability to "let go."

The Body's Armor

Lowen discussed two types of physical armoring of the control character defense. Individuals with this character defense are either seductive or overpowering. Seductive types are typically attractive and lead with being desirable in some way. They will be the image they are attached to, so if an athletic image is desirable, they will be athletic. If they believe being sweet and innocent is desirable, they will be sweet and innocent. They exert control through attractiveness in their interactions. Being physically attractive makes them safe and gives them a sense of control in their relationships.

This type has eyes that are soft and welcoming. Although they present as comfortable with sexuality, they rarely actually enjoy sexual intimacy fully.

For overpowering types, the upper body is typically highly defined while the lower body is usually thin and underdeveloped compared to the upper body. Think of a bodybuilder who skips leg day. Their ankles and calves are tight, and their shoulders will have a pulled-up appearance. They tend to have eyes that could pierce through you and are intense to gaze into. They are often physically intimidating.

Energetically, both types of this structure carry tension in the neck and shoulders. They very commonly have pain and tension at the base of the skull where it meets the neck. Lowen called it the "Head/Body Split," which disconnects the person's body from their emotions.

The Psychological Armoring

As mentioned before, the psychological armor of this character's defense is similar to traits of narcissistic personality disorder. This diagnosis carries a major stigma. I invite you to check in with yourself as you read about this type and acknowledge any feelings of judgment. Remember, with a great defensive pattern comes great pain. The ones who wear Control Armor carry deep fear and shame. They genuinely believe they are unsafe with others. Part of them feels less than human, so to protect themselves, they try to present as more than worthy and more than human. They believe this keeps them safer in connection with others.

These individuals believe they are untrustworthy, uncaring, and all-around terrible people. This armor guards against others believing that, but perpetuates the cycle when you get closer to them; their shame manifests through acting-out behaviors. They are in a constant war with themselves and often are labeled or will label themselves as "self-saboteurs." They will find themselves saying one thing and doing another, perpetuating the belief that they are inherently flawed at their core and can't be fixed.

A beautiful part of someone wearing Control Armor is that they are often brilliant. They spend their lives "in their heads," so they know a lot about many things. They are often inventors and innovators. They are interesting to talk to from an intellectual front, which is part of the allure of connection.

> Common Psychological Armoring Patterns Associated with Control Armor
>
> 1. I cannot trust anyone, including myself.
> 2. I must control others to feel powerful.
> 3. My emotions make me weak and vulnerable.
> 4. I am better off alone; others only disappoint me.
> 5. I must protect myself by remaining detached.
> 6. People are tools to be used for my gain.
> 7. Showing empathy or kindness makes me vulnerable.
> 8. I do not need anyone, and no one can be trusted.
> 9. I cannot allow myself to be influenced or controlled by anyone.
> 10. If I show weakness, I will be exploited.

The Energetic Armoring

The energy of someone wearing Control Armor is often friendly, cooperative, and pleasing. Their energy can feel sensual and intimate, as if they are pulling your energy into theirs. This may initially cause you to feel pulled to them with curiosity and excitement. Frequently, they pour energy into you when they first meet you, and sometimes throughout the connection. However, if they begin to feel your energy encroaching on theirs, they will withdraw their energy from the connection, feeling overwhelmed by the intimacy. Although they may not show it, their energy carries a slight anxiety, which can make you feel anxious around them.

Relationship Armoring

Relationships with this character's defense are often initially intense but short-lived or chaotic as time passes. This occurs in both friendships and romantic relationships. As intimacy builds, the individual will start to act out to show their partner who they truly believe they are and see if they are loved or rejected. Their armor requires them to prove to themselves that they are in control of all aspects of the relationship, which often involves not respecting boundaries in relationships. This often leads to a push-pull dance in which the one wearing Control Armor pushes away their partner and then pulls them back to prove to themselves they have power and are not in danger despite the intimacy that they are building. They will overanalyze their partner's actions, feelings, and thoughts, and may become psychologically invasive because they will believe they know their partner better than their partner knows themselves. They intend to feel safe, which means they must have power over their partner; however, they frequently harm their partner in the process, which only furthers their core belief that they are terrible.

Sam and Angie came to me for couples therapy, both reporting a lack of physical and emotional connection. They reported being "fine" most of the time, but then had arguments that would get so intense, Angie would scream and throw things.

> Note: When doing couples work, I also see members of the couple individually for some sessions. Doing so helps me gain a deeper understanding of them as individuals and how they interact in the dynamic of the relationship.

Individually, Sam would tell me all his theories about why Angie would get so angry. He didn't make himself out to be a victim, but rather treated the whole situation as if it were no big deal and nothing to be alarmed about. Angie was immensely remorseful and shame-ridden when we processed this pattern in individual sessions. In our couples sessions, both partners seemed to feel the behavior was not okay and wanted to ensure that I knew that it was something in the dynamic, not "Angie's fault." Sam wanted me to know this because being a victim of anything is entirely against his armoring pattern; for Angie, it was because she felt shame.

Eventually, Angie shared in a couples session that Sam had been unfaithful for their whole marriage, and that was why she was angry. Sam made her agree not to talk about this in our sessions, but she felt she had to because she believed it to be relevant, even if Sam said it wasn't. However, due to many conversations with Sam, she had begun to believe she was angry due to her childhood trauma, not the hurt she was feeling in her relationship. She was deeply confused about what she felt, and what Sam said made so much sense to her. As Angie shared this, Sam began to wring his hands, but a smile stayed on his face. The façade began to leave the session, and this is when we started to actually work.

We did a lot of work with this over our sessions. We did talk therapy and bioenergetics couples work. During the bioenergetic work, Angie became emotional. She would have tears in her eyes and feel anxiety in her chest. Sam would smile at her; he appeared to be looking through her.

"I think you are feeling these emotions because of some of your past relationships. It's obvious I love you so much, so I think you will agree it doesn't make sense to feel this way towards me," Sam would begin.

As Angie processed, she replied, "I just don't think he sees me. I don't feel he is truly connecting with me. I can't feel compassion. I am sitting here crying, and he just smiles at me. He tells me how I am feeling rather than asking. He doesn't get it! I want him to understand that he hurt me. If this continues, I will become so enraged that I will lose it!"

"I am feeling happy to be here with you! Isn't that enough? I am smiling," Sam retorted.

"What are you feeling in your body, Sam?" I asked.

"A smile, I am feeling a smile."

"I'm talking about emotion. What emotion are you feeling?"

"Happiness, obviously."

"Okay, great," I replied. "Where do you feel that in your body?"

Sam fell quiet.

For many individual sessions, we worked long and hard using both psychoeducation and Bioenergetics therapy. Sam shared his story with me about how his father would abuse him and his mother. Over time, he started to comfort his mom by joking and smiling with her to help her feel better, even after his own abuse. He learned to protect himself from the abuse by lying to his father and telling him things he wanted to hear. As a child, Sam felt immense empathy for his mom, and it often caused him to step in when his father was going to be abusive to her; he would take the abuse instead. The times when he couldn't step in and his mother was harmed, he felt immense shame and guilt.

His father would always take Sam out for a special bonding adventure after the worst of the abuse. Sam shared some confusion about this, even as he processed it as an adult. He didn't know how to feel about his father. He saw his father's pain, he felt his mother's pain, and he felt responsible for all of it. It was too much, so his brain adapted by shutting off the ability to truly feel empathy entirely.

We worked with letting go into his feelings and his breath. He processed immense fear, sadness, and disappointment from his childhood. He developed empathy for himself again. In time, he began to feel again. He described it as melting the ice he was living in. I could see the "ice" melt in his body as the tension slowly fell away. His relationship improved because he went from trying to understand his partner's feelings to feeling his own in response to hers. We have seen each other for about eight years now. I still see them both individually and as a couple. They continue to grow.

Enneagram Comparison

Someone wearing Control Armor would be most similar to the Enneagram Type 8 (the Challenger).

The core motivation of Eights is the fear of being controlled or harmed; thus, they seek to be powerful, independent, and in control of their environment. Someone wearing Control Armor and an Eight exhibits assertive, forceful behaviors to maintain control and protect themselves from vulnerability. Often, someone wearing Control Armor seems to lack emotional connection and empathy. At the same time, Eights are more likely to channel their aggression to protect those they care about, albeit in a more direct manner.

The Healing

The healing process for someone wearing Control Armor involves addressing deep-rooted shame due to perceived emotional and relational deficits, as well as breaking down defensive patterns that foster emotional detachment, manipulation, and lack of empathy. Individuals who carry this armor often exhibit traits such as emotional coldness, impulsivity, superficial charm, and a profound disconnection from their own emotions and bodily sensations. Control Armor tends to present with a rigid, controlled body posture, often associated with a lack of spontaneous expression and suppression of vulnerability.

Therapy for this armoring pattern begins with helping the individual reconnect with their body and become more attuned to bodily sensations, which are often disconnected due to the history of emotional neglect or trauma. We begin with grounding exercises, then move to body awareness, and gradually allow the person to feel a broader range of emotions, particularly fear, shame, and sadness—emotions they may have learned to avoid or suppress. We achieve this through deep breathing techniques, movement, and sometimes, expressive bodywork to loosen tension in the body, especially around the chest, throat, and pelvis.

In addition to bodywork, healing involves confronting the underlying lack of empathy and building a greater capacity for emotional awareness and connection with others. The therapist works with the individual to explore their early experiences and the relational dynamics that led to emotional detachment or callousness. This may include addressing childhood neglect, abandonment, or trauma and developing healthier emotional responses. This process involves gradually learning to express vulnerability and self-compassion. Developing true somatic self-compassion will allow them to access more compassion for others, leading to the development of genuine empathetic relationships.

Healing is a gradual process, as individuals with this defensive pattern may resist emotional engagement due to their deeply ingrained defenses. Many individuals with this armor have described dread and panic coming to sessions because of the risk of vulnerability once they enter a healing space. However, with consistent safety and invitation, the person can reconnect with their authentic emotions and build a more integrated sense of self, ultimately fostering healthier connections to themselves and others.

Beliefs to Be Reached Through the Healing Journey

1. It is safe for me to trust others and open up to connection.
2. I am powerful and capable without needing to control others.
3. I embrace my emotions as a source of strength and clarity.
4. I can experience vulnerability without fear of harm.
5. I choose healthy relationships based on mutual respect and trust.
6. I am worthy of kindness, and it is safe to be kind to others.
7. I release the need to remain detached from my feelings.
8. I trust myself to make healthy decisions and form genuine connections.
9. It is safe to let go of control and allow life to flow.
10. I am open to emotional intimacy and receiving love from others.

CHAPTER 8

PERFECTION ARMOR

Once we give up our true self to play a role, we are fated to be rejected because we have already rejected ourselves. Yet we will struggle to make the role more successful, hoping to overcome our fate but finding ourselves more enmeshed in it. We are caught in a vicious cycle that keeps closing in, diminishing our life and being.

—Dr. Alexander Lowen

Perfection Armor is perfectly designed, presented, and compressed by a large amount of pressure. It is typically built to defend against abandonment and rejection that typically occurs between the ages of four and eight. Perfection is an impossible goal for us humans; we are inherently imperfect from birth to death. This seems apparent, but it is surprising how much many of us struggle with this concept. So many of my clients, colleagues, and my own inner demons demand a degree of perfection from themselves and others. Someone with perfection armor requires perfection in order to function and feel safe in work, life, and relationships, and because perfection is never achievable, they never feel safe.

Someone wearing perfection armor, known as the rigid character structure in Lowen's terms, has trauma typically from four to seven years old. The trauma derives from feeling a sense of loss or physical rejection by at least one parent as

Perfection Armor

the child begins to become autonomous and independent, including having their own emotional and physical impulses. You are in a relationship with your parents, and navigating the complexities of this relationship can be difficult for the parents and child as the children begin to separate from the parent. The relationship evolves immensely during this stage of development.

Children love their parents more than anything. Their parents are their whole world, and their parents' approval means everything to them. They want nothing more than to make their parents happy and be loved by their parents for doing so. They want to feel physically close but not invaded by them. They want to feel emotionally connected but not emotionally controlled. Our children start to explore how to interact with us within their own unique selves and bodies.

One common way this armoring pattern forms is when our children begin to become sexual beings. During this stage of development, parents may unconsciously pull away physically from children due to their own discomfort. They stop responding to the child's physical needs for closeness, and they don't know how to handle the child's new need for physical boundaries. This distancing occurs even if the parents and child enjoyed initial intimacy and closeness; however, the relationship shifts when the children enter this developmental stage. This distance can lead them to believe their parents are rejecting them.

> **Children want nothing more than to make their parents happy and be loved by their parents for doing so.**

As adults, we frame physical intimacy as the physical pleasure we experience with our partners, and intimacy becomes inherently sexual due to this confusion. This view can cause parents to pull away physically from their children as they get older and become sexual beings. They stop holding hands, cuddling their child close, and holding them when they cry. Another example of how this armoring pattern can develop is that parents are overly possessive of children's bodies. They don't give them physical autonomy as they begin to desire and need it more intensely during this developmental stage.

At around age three or four, children will start to exert their physical boundaries and their physical needs because as they develop sexuality, they also develop a deep need for body autonomy and control. That is a good thing! They need parents to set appropriate boundaries, respect their boundaries, and allow healthy physical intimacy. This teaches them to follow their body's natural impulses, whether it be to connect or set a boundary. It connects their body's impulses to feelings of love and connection with others. Other common traumas that can cause this armoring pattern involve parents continuously criticizing or praising the way a child's body looks. Other factors can be the loss of a loved one, especially a parent or caregiver, and chaos and instability.

I will restate again and again that physical touch and intimacy are not inherently sexual; it is an important and somatic way of comfort and connection with those around us. I see sex taking over physical intimacy all the time and ruining marriages as one partner stops touching their partner at all due to them feeling like it only leads to sex; similarly, parents experiencing this developmental stage of their children stop touching them because it makes them uncomfortable. We need to normalize non-sexual physical intimacy because both our physical and mental health depend on it.

We need to normalize non-sexual physical intimacy because both our physical and mental health depend on it.

I have heard parents descriptively call the four-year-old stage the "Ferocious Fours." Four-year-olds can be ferocious, and they should be! At this stage, they ask themselves, "Does my parent love me if I am difficult or messy? Will they work to meet my needs even when it is hard?" Due to the need for acceptance from their parent at this age, any **chronic** feeling of rejection can lead to this armoring pattern.

Someone wearing Perfection Armor struggles with any kind of imperfection they may show. They carry immense pressure to perform and perform perfectly. They often feel pressured to look immaculate and speak eloquently. They may review an email multiple times before sending it. Any criticism leads to immense shame and often a deep emotional reaction. They also tend to hold others to extremely high standards and may be somewhat critical and rigid in their interactions. These individuals are extremely organized, principled, responsible, disciplined, and highly focused, sometimes to their detriment.

My client, Stasia, is an excellent example of someone wearing Perfection Armor. Stasia reported significant anxiety and deep depressive episodes in which she feels worthless and useless. She shared that she "tries so hard" and "gives everything to everybody," but still feels people don't want to know or connect with her. She feels people are disgusted by her.

Stasia was thin and rigid in her body. Her face was nearly frozen into a perfect smile. She smiled even while describing her deepest pain. Through bioenergetic training, it was easy to see that Stasia was cut off from her impulse to feel anything. She was in my office to be the best client she could so she could earn my willingness to work with her. She showed up to each session with a notebook and wrote down nearly every word I said.

Right away, we began breathwork and working with her emotions. We started on "begin messy," which brought up a tremendous fear of abandonment. One day, Stasia shared through processing that she had a deep longing in her body for connection with her father. She felt deep despair and missed him. When she was around five, her father went through a deep depression and withdrew from the family. He spent a tremendous amount of time in his room and began to deny her requests for connection, whether it be to watch a movie, go to the park, or cuddle. Her father passed away a year later. She remembered feeling confused and rejected, and she felt shame.

Stasia felt she wasn't good enough for her father. We see this emotion in children because they are extremely ego-centric, meaning what happens around them feels related to them directly. Children process the events that occur around them through the lens of responsibility and ownership. Although there was no direct intentional shaming related to Stasia, this armoring pattern developed.

The Body's Armor

Someone wearing Perfection Armor frequently holds their pelvis back. They breathe shallow into their chest; sometimes their breath is so shallow it is barely noticeable. Their eyes tend to be opened wider, as if they are intently looking for your expectations so they can meet them. They usually have their feet solidly planted on the ground with weight in their heels. Someone with this armoring pattern tends to be more invested in their ego image than in who they truly are. So, as someone connecting with them, you will feel a lot of energy, but it will manifest in anxiety.

This person is anxious about meeting environmental expectations so they can continue to project their perfection as much as possible. Due to this, Perfection Armor often presents with an idealized body according to societal standards. This standard applies to men and women, so body types also differ. Frequently, women are fit or thin, have feminine facial features, and are usually well-kept. They usually lead in relationships with their attractiveness and sexuality, so for some, they may appear hypersexual in how they walk, talk, and dress. Men are somewhat lean and muscular, with broad shoulders and sharp masculine facial features. Even their focus related to their body tends to be around the idea of perfection.

The Psychological Armoring

Individuals who wear Perfection Armor need to be perfect and defend themselves psychologically by thinking that if they work harder, they will be loved. If they perfect themselves, they will no longer be in danger of rejection, pain, or hurt. Their need to be perfect infiltrates their lives, whether they are writing an email or organizing their home. One client of mine would reread his emails up to ten times to ensure they didn't contain a grammatical error. Another was so focused on making sure her makeup was perfect that it would take her over an hour and several tries to feel it was complete.

Clients with this defensive pattern may also present with eating disorders, not due to feeling underserving of food, but because they feel the need to find the perfect body structure, which, for women in particular, means being thin. They think having extra weight may lead to rejection, which they can't risk. Self-hatred is a deep wound underneath the armor of perfection.

> Common Psychological Armoring Patterns Associated with Perfection Armor
>
> 1. I must be perfect to be accepted.
> 2. I am only valuable if I am in control.
> 3. I cannot show weakness or vulnerability.
> 4. I must control my emotions at all costs.
> 5. I will be rejected or punished if I make a mistake.
> 6. I must always be responsible and never let my guard down.
> 7. I cannot express myself freely without criticism.
> 8. I must avoid chaos, even if it means suppressing my true feelings.
> 9. I am weak if I relax or let go.
> 10. I am only worthy if I follow the rules and maintain order.

The Energetic Armoring

The energy of someone wearing Perfection Armor can easily be described as desperation. You may feel the person's desperation to please you and get everything right to avoid rejection. Their energy is very anxious, and a hint of anger/resentment is often present. This represents the split between the two needs: being loved for who they are and feeling they can only be loved if they aren't who they are.

Relationship Armoring

These individuals tend to separate love and sex and will cultivate relationships with those who can't truly love them, such as a married individual. They may feel overwhelmed with physical intimacy in relationships where they love the person because they are afraid to perform poorly. This causes them not to enjoy their own sexual pleasure. They will often feel upset with their partners for not being perfect and meeting their needs because they "try so hard." They will oscillate between that belief and then shame over how they are not doing a good enough job to earn their partner's love; this cycle leads to depressive episodes and self-hatred. Their deepest desire in a relationship is to be granted permission to fully accept themselves *and* be fully accepted by the person they love.

Enneagram Comparison

Someone wearing Perfection Armor is most similar to the Enneagram Type 1 (the Reformer).

The core motivation of the Enneagram One is the fear of being wrong or defective, which leads to a strong internal drive to be perfect and to uphold high moral standards.

Individuals wearing Perfection Armor and Ones strive for control and self-discipline to avoid emotional chaos or perceived moral failure. They also suppress emotions to maintain order. Ones are typically more focused on perfectionism in behavior and morality, whereas someone wearing Perfection Armor may be more concerned with emotional self-regulation and avoiding vulnerability.

The Healing

The healing process for someone donned in Perfection Armor focuses on loosening deep emotional and muscular tensions that reflect a strong need for control, perfectionism, and emotional restraint. As mentioned, individuals with this armoring often have a tightly controlled body, marked by muscular tension in areas such as the jaw, neck, back, and diaphragm. They tend to suppress emotions, particularly vulnerability, anger, and fear, often presenting with a calm, stoic exterior that masks underlying anxiety or frustration.

To reduce this armoring, we begin by addressing the physical tension through bodywork, such as deep breathing exercises, movement, and physical grounding techniques. These interventions help the individuals become more aware of the tension in their bodies and release it gradually, allowing for a greater flow of energy and emotion. The therapist helps the clients recognize how their control over their body and emotions is tied to a fear of chaos, failure, or loss of control.

As the individual starts to experience more freedom in their body, therapy also involves exploring the underlying fears and beliefs that drive the rigid patterns, particularly the fear of being vulnerable or making mistakes. By gradually allowing themselves to express emotions like anger or sadness, the ones who have to be perfect begin to experience a sense of emotional release and safety in letting go of perfectionism. In time, this helps the person develop more flexibility, both in their body and emotional responses, leading to healthier ways of coping with stress and a more authentic, less defensive way of engaging with themselves and others.

Ultimately, healing involves cultivating greater self-acceptance and emotional flexibility, allowing the individual to release the need for constant control and find a balance between structure and spontaneity. It involves reteaching them to listen to and trust their body and its impulses without shame to help them make meaningful decisions in their lives.

Beliefs to Be Reached Through the Healing Journey

1. I am worthy of love and acceptance as I am, even with imperfections.
2. I can safely release control and trust the flow of life.
3. I embrace vulnerability as a strength rather than a weakness.
4. I can freely and authentically express my emotions.
5. I view my mistakes as growth opportunities, not reasons for rejection.
6. I can relax and be at ease while still remaining responsible.
7. I can safely release rigidity and experience the fullness of life.
8. I am learning to trust that flexibility brings balance and peace.
9. I am worthy, even when I am not perfect or in control.
10. I embrace both structure and spontaneity in my life.

CHAPTER 9

FACTORS THAT KEEP US ENLISTED

If being is what life is all about, why are we so afraid of it? Why is it so difficult for us to "let go and just be"?
—Dr. Alexander Lowen

I have noticed many key barriers to our freedom that create complexity in our ceasefire. When we are at war, we often have camaraderie with the soldiers around us. Whether they are part of our platoon, like our family, or just like-minded soldiers struggling in ways similar to how we are, recovery can feel lonely at first. Frequently, those who begin to explore the idea of freedom tend to be the disruptors, especially in their family units, because those who aren't free need to attack anything that challenges their armor. The war we face may be generations old, and those around us have no idea what it looks like to be a civilian, and it terrifies them. This fear creates conflict, distance, and sometimes, complete disconnection.

It is also important to address what healing is. Throughout the years, so many of my clients came to me to "be happy." That is my initial goal too. If being happy is what you want, you will get that through healing. However, you will also get sadness, anger, guilt, and many other emotions. This is because feeling authentically happy means you must have access to feeling. You can't select which feelings you have access to; you must welcome all of them. Primarily, healing means you have permission to be human again. You become free, as you were when born, to be yourself. You breathe deeply without constriction, move your body with freedom, and feel the vast array of emotions you carry with the ability to express them in healthy and open ways.

I often joke that I should warn clients when they begin deep-level healing that they may not receive their desired outcome. For example, initially, you wanted to save your marriage, but after doing this work, you discover your marriage is not what you desire. Instead, it was what you thought you should want. Maybe you wanted to find peace with your job, but you realize you can't stay stuck one more day doing it. Getting into your body may mean reaching painful conclusions because it involves being true to yourself again.

After an intense personal session during my four-year bioenergetic training program, I was driving home feeling loved and at peace. I was singing in my car and smiling ear to ear. As I turned onto the road to my house, my stomach began to knot. I dreaded going home to my former partner, and I began to panic. What did this mean? What should I do? Without any conscious effort, I took myself out of my body and began thinking there wasn't a reason to be scared or upset; I told myself that my partner was wonderful. I stopped feeling the emotion as I pulled into the driveway, not because I had resolved it, but because I was again out of my body. I had donned my armor of selflessness and resentment.

At that time, I could not deal with what my body felt. I felt a similar feeling in my belly whenever I did my own work and returned to my body. Like clockwork, I repressed and denied. Eventually, the relationship ended. I cried for the loss of the relationship, but more for the loss of myself. When I felt this emotion, I knew what it meant on some level, but I didn't want to recognize it.

As we heal, denying our truth becomes more difficult, and changes may have to be made. If not, our healing journey will stall until we are able to move forward in authentic connection with our body. Any situation that causes us to disconnect from our truth will impede our healing.

Healing doesn't always involve making drastic changes, but it may. Some clients conclude that they really hate their job, but instead of quitting, they decide to stay for the benefits. However, they stand in the truth of how much they hate it and practice extra self-care to honor their body's struggle in going against its will. Others decide to leave and seek employment elsewhere.

Somatic work involves coming home to your body, finding your truth instead of your idea of your truth, and creating a relationship with your body where you no longer ignore or betray it. It is the most arduous healing journey and requires regular practice and dedication, but it is also the most rewarding for our physical and mental health. Coming to therapy to process and deal with past events is highly beneficial. Unfortunately, pain doesn't live in the past; pain will be in our present and our future, so knowing how to process it naturally and organically is important. Not doing so will lead to a continuation of mental and physical diseases.

Somatic work is the most arduous healing journey and requires regular practice and dedication, but it is also the most rewarding for our physical and mental health.

What does this look like in real life? In sessions, it often looks like crying on the floor after opening to the sadness through breathwork or hitting a cube with a bat or racquet to release years of unexpressed feelings in the body, so healing can take place. The more trapped emotions that individuals release, the calmer they begin to feel day to day. They no longer have to work to calm themselves by changing or reframing their thoughts many times during the day. Being a human just becomes more manageable.

Now, reframing and changing or blocking thoughts are still relevant strategies and needed at times; my goal is to help clients utilize those skills minimally because they are in a safe and secure relationship with themselves, where they know how to comfort their emotions, not stop them. This looks like fully embracing vulnerability, authenticity, and finding peace within yourself by accepting your emotions as part of your life and human experience. It's crying on the floor without shame and being at peace with knowing and trusting your body is doing exactly what it needs. It's letting yourself go deeply into the emotion and knowing that it won't consume you, but it will free you.

At times, feeling your emotions may seem inconvenient. However, I equate it to using the restroom, getting a drink of water, or eating. Sometimes, you find it inconvenient to take care of your body when you have a million things to do, but it is necessary. If you have to use the restroom, you make space in your life to do so. If you need to drink water or eat, you find time to nourish yourself. Allowing emotional expression is simply another way to nourish yourself. It is a release mechanism ingrained in our biology, just like any other bodily function. You deserve peace within your body—achieving this peace should be a top priority for all of us.

The Manufacturer of Our Armor: The Ego

Our ego and ego defense are huge barriers to our natural healing process. The ego manufactures our armor. It is the part of us that cares about us above all else. It is our ultimate protective force, but can also be our downfall. Our egos protect us in conscious and unconscious ways, suppressing our ability to be our true selves.

Think of toddlers. They have a lot of determination but no ego, in the way I mean it. They don't care how others perceive them as they learn new things, feel their emotions, or speak for what they want. I am not saying we should completely revert to being toddlers; I am saying we should have the ability to be as free as our inner toddlers, but with a prefrontal cortex to know when it is safe to do so.

Internally, many of us are as messy as a toddler crying in the grocery store when he doesn't get the candy he wanted. We just don't allow ourselves to feel sad or disappointed in a situation because our prefrontal cortex tells us we don't have a right to that feeling. Your emotions and your body don't care what you have a "right" to feel; they simply feel. I invite you to check in even as you read this comparison. Has your ego been activated? Do you resent the idea of being in any way compared to a toddler? If so, that is your ego.

Clearly, I am not saying you should throw a tantrum in the grocery store. However, I think that could be a great scene for a movie where everyone else feeling similar frustrations follows suit. We should and can have a relationship with ourselves where we internally validate even the smallest of feelings. "It sucks not to get what I want!" Saying that to yourself in your head is all it takes in a minor emotional situation to leave you feeling validated, heard, and connected. If the emotion is more intense than a typical day-to-day struggle, it may require more extensive validation and release from the body.

I have seen the power of validation directly with my toddlers. When I validate what they are struggling with, saying something like, "It is so hard to have to leave the playground when you want to keep playing." I instantly can see that their bodies relax. Feeling understood translates to feeling safe.

Another way the ego impedes our healing process is through ego dreams versus soul dreams. As they do this work, sometimes individuals realize they cannot be true to themselves in their current life. They are likely living in their "ego dreams." Ego dreams are the dreams we have for ourselves and our lives that come from what we think we are supposed to do. They can range from getting married and having children to becoming a doctor to buying a two-million-dollar home and a Tesla.

Ego dreams feel good because we know we are perceived positively. They are not bad, and it is not a bad thing to follow your ego dreams. However, these dreams will never make you genuinely happy. They will let you feel happy for a moment, but soon, your ego will become unsatisfied, and you will need to find another accomplishment or impressive thing to do. The new car will just become your car. The new home will become old news in your friend group. It will no longer serve your ego and, therefore, no longer be a dream.

A soul dream is a dream that is all for you. It feels peaceful in your body. It helps you feel good in your life, and that is the intention. These dreams rarely have anything to do with material items, although they can. They are calm and not anxiety-based. They exist in the quiet of your mind and heart. They make you wake up in the morning wanting nothing but this moment. This doesn't mean you stop reaching for ego dreams or goals. Instead, it means you don't *need* to accomplish them to be happy anymore. Your soul is settled. You are free.

A soul dream feels peaceful in your body and helps you feel good in your life.

Permission to Feel

Being granted permission to feel is a complex part of trauma recovery. Anyone with trauma has, in some way, been told they do not have permission to feel the trauma's effects. Often, individuals who enter my office carry immense fear and shame related to emotional expression. We have to process through this in order to access permission to feel and process the trauma underneath their mental health symptoms. Post-traumatic stress disorder develops when we cannot emotionally process the event that caused the trauma.

As we begin the process of trauma recovery, we get in touch with intense emotions, like hatred and despair, and it feels wrong to feel them. Often, we will create a narrative about why we shouldn't feel this way rather than accepting our body's truth of how it feels. Our feelings do not hurt anyone. I promise you that yelling in my office about how much you hate your sibling/mother/father/spouse while you beat my foam cube to release the anger from your body will not harm them. They are not listening. However, holding that energy in *will* harm you. Without full permission to feel in safe spaces, we will continue to hold onto tension both somatically and psychologically. As mentioned previously, this can cause mental health disorders and even physical disease.

If you have a feeling you "just can't shake," it is likely you don't know the feeling to the extent it needs to be known and haven't granted it permission to be expressed. In my office, all feelings are welcome, and once they are released, we have a clear picture of what to do. Feelings don't mean action, they mean feeling, so we can have more clarity over the action that needs to take place.

Some clients come in, go over to the bioenergetic stool, and cry deeply about not loving their partner anymore. In the next session, they say that they have had the best week with their spouse. They feel closer than ever; they feel like they have broken through a wall, and they see their spouse for the first time in a long time. They just needed to allow themselves to feel the fear and despair of not loving their spouse anymore. Once they move through that emotion, they understand that those feelings were not about their spouse at all. The feelings may have been projected onto their spouse, but were about something deeper. Until we let ourselves truly and fully feel, we can't allow ourselves to process our truth.

I have also experienced the opposite: clients come in with peace and clarity that they need to get divorced. We can't know what the permission to feel will lead to, so we avoid it. However, I do know it helps us lead us to our truth.[19]

Pain is not bad. It isn't an enemy; it is a signal to the brain that something is not right. If you have a broken bone, I want you to feel pain; it's dangerous if you don't. If it is a broken leg, I want you to know not to walk on your leg. I want you to be gentle with yourself, so you don't feel shooting pain. I don't want you to push through the pain or ignore it and cause more harm.

> **Until we let ourselves truly and fully feel, we can't allow ourselves to process our truth.**

This is similar to emotional pain. Normalizing and denying pain is dangerous. Eventually, pushing through trauma can kill people, either through physical or mental illness. These armoring patterns lead to a lifetime of denial in your mind and body. If you don't address them, they will lead to physical and emotional pain.

As I discussed in chapter 1, many clients struggle with physical illness, in which they seek medical care and their physicians send them to me after not being able to find a purely physical cause for the symptoms they are experiencing. The clients are perhaps not aware of any emotional struggles. I have seen their frustration; they suffer from physiological symptoms, such as gastrointestinal issues, heart palpitations, chronic migraines, and so much more, but they do not understand why.

When their physicians tell them to manage their stress or that their symptoms could be trauma-related, the client becomes outraged. They say, "This is not all in my head!" as if the doctor were saying their symptoms weren't real. They are outraged because they believe in the misconception that mental health separates us from physical health.

Dramatically and plainly put, trauma disorders are a disease of the body that impacts your physical and mental health. Trauma is real and causes physical symptoms, and physicians will tell you this. They are not telling you that your symptoms are less physically real than any other disease. In fact, studies show that someone with childhood trauma is 2 to 2.3 times more likely to have strokes, cancer, and/or heart disease, 3.2 times more likely to have chronic lower lung disease, and 1.4 times more likely to experience diabetes.[20] You should absolutely treat trauma like any other physical disease by seeking a medical doctor's help managing the physical symptoms, and you should also treat underlying trauma with the help of a therapist, preferably through some sort of somatic work that includes the body, although talk therapy can also be highly beneficial.

Fear of Connection and Comfort

It may surprise you how much pushback I get with the topic of connection. I always share that connection is one of the foundational pillars to healing physically and mentally for all of us. So many come to me wanting to figure out how to do this independently, and they can't. You need others in your life to support, hold, teach, and care for you.

I understand why people look at me as if I ate their piece of cake when I say this. Connection has been painful and will continue to be painful at times. That is almost always why individuals come to see me. What caused them to be here is also the thing that will set them free.

Connections are painful because they matter. The pain you have experienced in the past through connection can and should be healed. However, even during or after therapy, if you have a relationship of any sort, there will be moments where it hurts. This is because we are challenged in connections. Relationships with others hold mirrors to us. They constantly show us who we are by how we interact with them. Our imperfect parts will come out. If you are insecure, that will come into the connection. If you are jealous, that emotion will enter the connection. If you feel unlovable, you will eventually experience that in the connection.

We are biologically designed to need connections from birth to death. From the moment we are born, connection keeps us alive. If we don't have a connection with our caregivers, we will not survive. The famous Romanian orphan study demonstrated this. At one time, many Romanian officials adamantly believed orphans had innate behavioral problems, and they left children in orphanages because of these problems. Over one hundred Romanian orphans were left in an orphanage or put in foster care. Those in foster care fared far better than those in orphanages. A study involving these Romanian orphanages investigated whether a lack of love and connection can kill. This study found that babies who experienced isolation and a lack of love/connection were significantly more likely to grow slower, contract illnesses, and die early.[21]

> **Relationships with others hold mirrors to us. They constantly show us who we are by how we interact with them.**

Countless studies demonstrate that connection is key to our physical and mental health. Studies show loneliness can account for a 29 percent to your chances of having coronary artery disease and a 39 percent increase in your likelihood to have a stroke.[22] This is just one of many staggering statistics to demonstrate the importance of connection. A study examining how connection impacts depressed individuals found that depressed individuals who made social connections decreased the likelihood for depressive relapse by 24–63 percent depending on social connection before the experiment and the number of connections formed during the study.[23]

Our world is becoming less and less connected. Connection is not only going to lunch with a friend; it is deeper than that. Connection that positively impacts mental and physical health must have somatic and emotional components. People report to me that being around others raises their blood pressure or makes them more anxious, not less! They will also share that they feel better alone. This results because the connections don't have the comforting components of emotionally safe and connected relationships.

I am not saying that it's enough to sit by each other at a restaurant; I am citing the importance of meaningful connections. People who give you long hugs when you need them and hold you as you cry. Connections that you run to when something is wrong or when you want to celebrate something going right. We need people who meet our emotional and physical needs for connection. Our body needs to *feel* connected to others. A hand on a shoulder, eye contact, and even holding hands can lower blood pressure and cause us to breathe more deeply. This is biologically wired into us, which is why, as young children, we run to our mothers for closeness and comfort.

Our body needs to *feel* connected to others.

Many of us are terrified of rejection deep down. Ultimately, all of the armoring patterns in this book are to guard against rejection and disconnection. Rejection is neurobiologically one of the biggest fears of life. Therefore, connecting has become complex and scary, which leads us to want to deny its importance and avoid it. We have found a cheat code that satiates the need to connect in our brains by interacting on social media. This is a connection of the mind, not of the body. These connections cannot satiate the actual need for connection; they give us a false sense of the need being met with minimal risk. We are addicted to this type of connection because, at the moment, it feels like it satiates our need for it. However, a few moments after we log off, we realize we need another hit. Social media has led to perhaps the greatest social isolation epidemic of our time because we settle for that connection rather than seeking what our body truly craves.

Substance Abuse

Drugs and alcohol are another way we separate from connection with others and from ourselves and our emotional truth. When I worked in an inpatient substance abuse unit, I learned perhaps some of the most important lessons of my career. I began a bioenergetics group, which many at the facility thought would never work. They told me that individuals on the unit would not be interested in such intense and emotional therapy methods, which made me feel nervous about starting the group. Would I push them to the point where they would want to go back to using? Would anyone show up?

To this day, what happened in those groups gives me goosebumps. Not only did people show up, but the line was out the door and I could only allow in a specific number of people. It didn't push individuals to use, and they reported less desire to use ever again. I still have clients from those groups reach out to me, reporting that their sobriety was a byproduct of those groups and the deep healing that occurred through the connections formed there. I admit that this isn't true for all of the group members; some went back to using and died, some are still using, and some are still fighting for their sobriety. However, of all the methods I utilized, somatic therapy, which focuses on connection and feeling even the most intense emotions, seemed to be the most powerful.

I remember not knowing why this worked so well in graduate school, but hearing a quote later on made by Johann Hari on a TED talk made me realize it. He said, "The opposite of addiction isn't sobriety, it is connection." This made so much sense to me, and it is what I witnessed in the groups. The famous Rat Park study demonstrated empirically that social connection led to less substance abuse and addiction.[24] In the study, water was laced with morphine, which is extremely addictive. The study found that rats in socially enriching environments were less likely to utilize the morphine laced water than those in socially isolated environments.

Drugs and alcohol don't improve our lives. They don't meet our needs; they give us a false sense of somatic comfort for a moment until it wears off, and we realize we are where we were before or even worse off. I have seen individuals trade their connection with their kids, spouse, or friends for their connection with a drug or alcohol. This isn't a choice. It is because they can numb their need for people and separate from their emotional pain. They are now in control of when they feel comfort and don't have to engage with the vulnerability of relying on others to meet their needs.

We live in a society where we prefer to numb our feelings rather than feel them. We numb our sadness rather than be vulnerable and connect with others. However, my full calendar means that some people don't want to live this way; we seek truth, connection, and peace within ourselves without needing to numb ourselves with drugs, dissociative activities, and/or character defenses. Every day, the individuals, couples, and families I work with inspire me. They show up when life is hard. They resist but persist. I am truly humbled to be a part of this journey to deeper connections.

The Concept of Forgiveness

Forgiveness is probably one of the most commonly used words, but the most complex concept in my work with clients. Many religious ideas of forgiveness are based on the mind "overcoming" the pain and anger that an individual carries, which helps many people believe they can move on by simply choosing to forgive. In my experience, this is not true forgiveness, and it does nothing for the muscular tension and emotion carried in the body. Forgiveness has to look different to allow the person's body to not carry the lack of forgiveness in the form of rigidity, chronic pain, and mental/physical disease. It requires the release of the harm caused from the body.

The logical mind might forgive when told, but the body is not so easily convinced. Forgiveness in the body requires the individual to feel safe again after being harmed. This may mean cutting contact with the person who harmed them, so they are now safe. It can look like setting boundaries or going to therapy. The body needs to know that it will not be harmed again if it relaxes. If you think about it, forgiving and continuing to have someone in your life who hasn't changed their behavior or isn't apologetic is evolutionarily a poor choice and is highly complicated. This doesn't mean you have to carry emotions related to the harm you endured; you can release those, but you don't have to reach peace with the person who harmed you.

However, not reaching peace with that person means we cannot "let it go" emotionally. For example, many of us have been up until 3:00 a.m. talking in circles with our partners, trying to feel differently but saying the same things over and over. This is because the mind may understand the argument but the body and emotional mind are still experiencing fear and guardedness. The only thing that can cause that safety to allow the body to relax and true somatic forgiveness is feeling safety within connection again.

Individuals who have been abused, neglected, invalidated, or harmed and have not done the work to be safe cannot truly forgive their abuser in a somatic sense. They will feel their nervous system activate around the person who harmed them. The body will hold tension and fear. If someone remains in connection with those who caused them harm, they will need to learn to express and set boundaries in order to be safe. They will also need to choose themselves internally or sometimes externally over those who harmed them as part of their healing process. To do this, they must set boundaries and stand in their truth with these individuals, not necessarily with anger or malice towards the individual, but in love for themselves.

I often describe forgiveness as imagining you have your inner child standing behind you in each of these interactions. Your inner child wants to connect with the person in front of them, but may need your help in setting boundaries and speaking up for her or him in a way they are unable. Becoming your own healthy parent is one of the ultimate goals of therapy for those healing from childhood trauma. Reparenting yourself is a crucial part of the recovery journey. It's not something you should have to do, but it is often necessary for lasting healing. Learning to protect yourself in the ways you weren't protected, to love yourself in the ways you weren't loved, and to understand yourself in the ways you were never understood is how you begin to move forward.

It is important to note that those who harmed us carry their own pain and trauma. In family systems, the trauma is often intergenerational. It is absolutely important to process and understand this. It may lead to individuals having empathy for those who harmed them, which can be extremely healing. However, the empathy for those who harmed us can not come before the empathy for ourselves. I frequently see clients who minimize their abuse by understanding the stories of their abusers. In most cases, this does not constitute true forgiveness; it constitutes a method of repression.

It is also important to note that as you read this book, you may begin to understand current and past partners, friends, and family members who have hurt you or continue to cause you harm. Your understanding and empathizing with the person you see underneath the armor does not mean they will disarm or become safe for you. They must do their work to disarm, and they must authentically want to. This healing work is too difficult to do if someone is not all in. It is okay to have empathy for their struggles and their healing journey, but it is important not to take responsibility for it.

The Fear of Taking Off Our Armor

I have come to realize that people are tremendously fearful of freedom. The armor we wear absolutely limits us, but it also protects us in a world where we unfortunately find ourselves needing protection. Any trauma survivor needs to know they can access armor as needed. Life has proven to be unpredictable when it comes to laying down maladaptive armor with no alternative protection. Healing in our culture involves finding a balance in which we are armored and free. We are meant to carry some kind of armor. Our brain never stops having the fight, flight, and freeze mechanism. This will be with us throughout our lifetime, and it should be.

Even with all the therapy and all the healing, we will find ourselves armoring up. You will feel your jaw tighten during a tense meeting as you hold back anger. You will feel your shoulders rise in an argument with your spouse. This isn't a bad thing, and this armoring should be temporary. I encourage you to be aware that this armoring occurs, so you can release it again when it is safe to do so. You will slow down and remind yourself that you are safe with yourself, and therefore, you are safe.

Part of reading this book helps you don the armor of knowledge and inspires reconnection with the wisdom built into your body. To learn how your mind and body work, what you need, and most importantly, who you truly are. This new armor will allow you to minimize the amount of maladaptive armoring patterns you must utilize to soldier through life. Soldiering is an important part of life, and in some instances, causes us to live healthier and more productive lives. My hope is that you learn to soldier with different types of armor, such as self-compassion, boundaries, freedom to feel, and a desire to understand all parts of who you are. The most important goal is to feel safe with yourself, in your body and mind, and to trust yourself implicitly.

Finding healthy ways to armor, such as self-worth, good communication, and boundaries, will reduce the defensiveness you need in your mind and body. If you feel empowered to believe you deserve to be free, you will set boundaries of empowerment, not defensiveness. You will express your truth out of freedom, not desperation.

This is the ultimate balance we are seeking. It can take years of healing work to reach this place, and frequently, people give up on themselves too early. They become discouraged when their healing journey appears to be lagging. It took many years to build the armor. It may take many years to shed it, and keeping it off will take healing practices for the rest of your life. You will need to continue the activities that ground you in yourself and give you a feeling of safety in a world where we are all inherently unsafe.

Even after healing childhood trauma, life will continue to present us with difficulties. People you love will die, you will lose jobs, and you will face a variety of things designed to send you back to war. However, this time, you will be armed with awareness and self-love to help you navigate the challenges, making the wars temporary and intentional.

The Need for True and Authentic Safety

A problematic aspect of trauma recovery is that once you are a soldier, you can not lay down the armor until you are authentically safe. Many clients have questioned why they can't be like everyone and have relationships with people even if they don't like them, even if they don't feel safe with them. The truth is, you can! However, the relationship will be one that is defended and armored. You will be standing behind your armor, and connecting only in moments of safety.

Individuals who have had trauma need truth, authenticity, and emotional honesty to feel safe and have close and intimate relationships. Otherwise, it takes a lot of energy for them to connect because their soldiers are continually on duty. This is one of the reasons why individuals with trauma feel anxious about social events and may even limit them.

This often looks like a struggle or conflict in close relationships. There may be regular conflict in a relationship with someone with trauma, not because they are trying to push the person away, but because they are trying to find safety by pulling them close. This conflict tests how the relationship will navigate emotional struggles to establish whether the person feels safe.

The relationship doesn't have to be perfect to be authentic. It only needs to be safe to talk through emotions, difficulties, and other messy moments. If we can navigate the messiness of relationships, we can have authentic relationships. Individuals who have suffered from childhood trauma need to know it is possible to have intimacy in relationships and exist in them without armor.

Comparative Suffering

A prominent therapist and researcher, Brené Brown, described *comparative suffering* in her book *Daring Greatly*.[25] Competitive suffering describes comparing your pain, trauma, or circumstances to someone else's. Clients invalidate their trauma in a variety of ways. Some clients say their parents yelled and threw things but didn't hit them, so it "wasn't that bad." Others say that their parents didn't emotionally connect with them, but always had food on the table, so they should just be grateful for what they had.

It is important to remember that this idea of comparing trauma comes from the prefrontal cortex, the thinking part of your brain that loves to sort, categorize, and assign value. However, trauma doesn't live there, and that part has little say over what is important in trauma recovery. Our body, the speaker for our emotional brain, dictates how we feel. So, no matter what you think about your trauma, your body will feel the severity of the trauma you experienced, and remember, the body doesn't lie. As mentioned previously in this book, trauma is a physiological response that takes place in the brain following an event. If that physiological response occurs in the brain, then trauma has occurred, no matter what opinions we hold about the severity of the event.

Many parents use this invalidation technique to minimize or repress their children's feelings because they are uncomfortable with them. This technique leads to children feeling shame for having emotions because someone always "has it worse." I believe that this perspective of comparative suffering is a trauma perspective, coming from the idea that there is a scarcity of empathy and emotional understanding. We compete with others because the resources are scarce. Empathy should not be a scarce resource in our homes or in society.

No matter our diagnosis, past experiences, race, gender identity, or any other aspect of self that may be separating us, what connects us is our human needs. At the very least, we all need and deserve love, connection, safety, food, water, shelter, respect, and autonomy. We all deeply desire these aspects of life, and when these needs are not consistently met, we suffer.

Our suffering may be different, but I do not believe in creating an overall hierarchy of suffering because this elevates one person's need above another's. The only thing that creates a greater need is if we don't have enough. Scarcity is the issue, not who is suffering more. I understand some resources are scarce; however, there does not have to be scarcity related to needs such as empathy or respect. The competition for who is suffering more comes from the need for our suffering to be valid. Yes, your suffering is valid, but your needs are also valid, and so is your identity.

No matter our diagnosis, past experiences, race, gender identity, or any other aspect of self that may be separating us, what connects us is our human needs.

Struggling with Boundaries

Boundaries play a crucial role in the healing journey for those with complex post-traumatic stress disorder. Many individuals struggle with their sense of identity, needs, and desires after enduring childhood trauma because they were not allowed to express or acknowledge these aspects of themselves. As a result, they may not know what they truly think, feel, or want, because survival, not personal needs, was the priority during their childhood. Setting boundaries can range from something as simple as expressing how we feel to something more complex, like articulating what we need from others.

For example, many of my clients need to begin speaking their truth as part of their healing process, which may be difficult for their families to hear. A boundary might sound like, "It's hard for me to share this, so I need you to listen first and then respond." Or it could be, "I need clarity on how you feel because when I don't know, I feel unsafe." Sometimes, a boundary is as simple as, "I need you to understand that I felt hurt when you said you didn't want to share things with me." A boundary reflects your identity within a relationship—it's about taking up space as who you truly are and asking the other person to see and understand you. In many of the armoring patterns described in this book, a significant trauma for a child is their parent being threatened by the child's identity. As a result, individuals with CPTSD often believe that others will perceive their identity and needs as threats to them and the relationship. Setting boundaries with someone doesn't mean you don't love them; it means you are learning to love yourself.

> A boundary reflects your identity within a relationship—it's about taking up space as who you truly are and asking the other person to see and understand you.

Trauma Research Bias

One last barrier I want to share related to trauma recovery is specifically for those individuals who fall into minority categories. Trauma research has historically been limited in its representation of racial and gender minorities, often marginalizing these groups or failing to account for their unique trauma experiences. This lack of diversity in research samples leads to a significant gap in understanding how different communities experience and respond to trauma.

This oversight has implications for understanding how cultural, social, and historical contexts affect trauma experiences in these groups. LGBTQIA+ individuals have also been significantly underrepresented in trauma research, with studies failing to account for the distinct ways gender and sexual identity intersect with traumatic experiences. Furthermore, Crenshaw's work on intersectionality highlights how trauma research often neglects the complex interactions between race, gender, and other social identities, thereby limiting the scope of understanding in marginalized communities.[26]

Although most of the topics discussed in this book are meant to represent all individuals regardless of race, gender, sexual orientation, or religion, the book and most other research will have blind spots. It is important to acknowledge these gaps that suggest the need for more inclusive and intersectional approaches in trauma research to ensure that all populations' unique experiences are understood and addressed effectively. When working with an individual who may be underrepresented in the research, I still draw from what I know but acknowledge what I don't know as part of their treatment plan.

CHAPTER 10

CEASEFIRE

*It is only by making the past alive again for
a person that a true growth in the present is facilitated.
If the past is cut off, the future does not exist.*
—Dr. Alexander Lowen

Working through trauma can take years. Although some changes or differences may be felt after one session, sustainable peace and change can take years to accomplish. The trauma occurred over many years, so the healing may also need similar space and time, which is not a popular view in a culture that likes fast results.

Our journey with healing never fully ends. I have been working on myself for over 20 years, and I still find new parts of myself that need to be known. Through my work and watching the work of my clients, I have learned to release the idea that I need to rush toward healing. I teach my clients that as they go through their journey, they are healed, and they are in the process of healing. Both are true.

It can also take clients years of talk therapy before they are comfortable getting into somatic healing work. Many times, I have clients with whom I do talk therapy exclusively while sprinkling in somatic awareness when appropriate. Sometimes, I have clients do a sprinkle of somatic therapies but revert to talk therapy. An important part of this process is knowing there is no one way. We need to respect our armor as much as our emotions. Our armor will allow us to do the therapy we are ready for at any given time. We must respect that and wait until there is enough safety before moving forward.

It is important to note that, through my work, I have witnessed individuals change armoring patterns. Someone who starts with Elusive Armor may become more similar physiologically, energetically, and psychologically to the one wearing Need Armor as they do their healing work. Someone with Elusive Armor will likely go through all the physical armorings to different extents and for different lengths of time as a development process. Someone who starts in Endurance Armor is also likely to go through the preceding armoring patterns in their work.

Wherever our trauma is, we stopped developing fully at that particular point, so we will need to revisit the preceding developmental stages and reprocess them somatically and psychologically. I joke that we have to grow up through our therapy work when we have childhood trauma, that is, we will go through developmental stages we were unable to do in our childhood.

Tips for Moving Through Trauma

Trauma occurs when your brain gets stuck. People stop moving emotionally through the experience and cannot process it. So, healing trauma involves the individual moving through it. We must be able to access and activate the neural pathways, the part of ourselves where the trauma is, to encourage it to begin to move through processing and release. The suggestions here are designed to activate certain aspects of ourselves that often carry trauma. No single aspect of these suggestions and exercises will serve as a cure-all. They are recommendations and ideas to help you begin to find your individualized path back to your body, your health, and your freedom.

No exercise is "one size fits all." Adjustments may be needed to help you complete the exercise. It is never healthy to just do the exercise because you are told to; this can lead to dissociation or repression. You must be present in the exercise to be safe while doing the exercise. If you can not do the exercise without dissociation or if you feel forced, it is important to step back and share that with your somatic therapist. That may be what gets processed before any of what your therapist has planned.

These tips are meant to support healing, and the exercises are designed to help process emotions through the body. The truth is, until we allow ourselves to feel the trapped emotions from our trauma, we cannot truly heal. No amount of positive lifestyle changes or coping strategies can replace that. However, the following tips are somatic changes I've seen as beneficial in supporting a return to the body and assisting with processing our stories. These exercises may not lead to the rapid release of locked emotions, although for some, they have. However, they can start the process of reconnecting with your body, which will make major release easier later on. They can also support your release. I recommend these exercises to most clients to utilize in conjunction with the intense release we do in the office.

The truth is, until we allow ourselves to feel the trapped emotions from our trauma, we cannot truly heal.

One of the first recommendations I give anyone who comes into my office is to start moving their body. If you have ever watched an animal like a gazelle or zebra being chased by a lion and surviving, they instantly shake their body once they are safe. They are literally shaking off their fear. They shake off, loosen back up, and move forward. We don't do that; we tense up and move forward. Due to this, moving your body intentionally and with a desire to connect to it can be a great start to your trauma healing journey. Most of us live sedentary lives, which can negatively impact our overall health.

Now, when I say "move your body," I don't mean you have to run a marathon or do CrossFit—although, if that's what you decide to do, more power to you. What I mean is to move your body, whether it's going for a walk, stretching, shaking, swimming, dancing, or playing actively with your kids. I don't care how you do it. I recommend that anyone with trauma incorporate regular movement into their lives. The more trauma we store, the more rigid our bodies become, and we need to shake it off.

Walking

One of my personal favorite forms of movement is walking or running. If you do this, focus on each footstep as it lands. Concentrate on your steps and your breathing, and allow your mind to process the rest, whether consciously or unconsciously. It is best to breathe deeply in through your nose and loosen your jaw to breathe out through your mouth. If a specific memory arises, don't try to avoid it—simply walk with it. Bring your attention to your breathing, your steps, and any bodily sensations you experience as you walk with the memory. Allow both your mind and body to process the troubling memory through the bilateral stimulation of your movement. If emotion comes, let it.

Dancing

Putting on one of your favorite songs or a song that resonates with you on a particular day and allowing your body to move freely is a great way to get in touch with your body and its natural impulses. Try not to think too much about how you should move; just move in a way that feels good to your body. Don't focus on what may look good to others; no one else is around, this is just for you! It doesn't matter if the movements are big or small, graceful or more intense, quick or slow. Just allow your body to move. Notice any shame or resistance that comes up for you. When did it become shameful to move YOUR body even when you are alone? When did you lose the rights to your movement?

> **Important Note on Exercise**
>
> Exercise can only be healing if it's done in a healing manner. If you're exercising to change your body instead of connecting to it and accepting it, you're likely shaming your body, which will hinder the healing process. If you have an inner drill sergeant telling you that you're not pushing yourself hard enough or moving intensely enough, that's trauma influencing your movement. Exercise won't help you heal if it's rooted in punishment. For exercise to truly support healing, it must be done for the sake of your body, not to punish it. So, pay attention to your inner dialogue as you move your body.

Nutrition

Caring for your body through nutrition is another important way to support your healing journey. Many individuals struggle with their relationship with food. They may either restrict their intake or alternate between restricting and bingeing. They feel uncomfortable in their bodies, including with their physical appearance. When we haven't received comfort or know how to receive it, we turn to somatic comforting methods. Eating can provide comfort and fullness when our lives feel scary or empty, which can lead to not trusting our bodies and ignoring our hunger cues. Instead of learning to work with our hunger, we may villainize it. Rather than allowing our thinking brain to support and work with our hunger, we panic and try to repress it. This triggers an unconscious response to repress our thinking brain, which can lead to bingeing. It becomes a constant battle between the part of our brain that tries to nurture our body through food and our conscious brain telling us not to trust our hunger.

There are nutritionists trained in helping individuals with their healing journey through dietary support. Nutritionists can also help identify nutrients missing in the body that may be contributing to mental health concerns. For instance, certain nutrients are needed to support the creation of dopamine. If these nutrients are low or lacking, dopamine production will be low. Research suggests that nutrition should be a part of an individual's mental health journey.[27] Although a nutritionist is best to advise the approach for each individual, one of my favorite approaches to nutrition is intuitive eating. This involves relearning how to follow the voice of your body to nourish your body with food. It is a complex approach and too in-depth for this book. However, I recommend that people on a healing journey explore their relationship with food and see a nutritionist to reclaim freedom with food and eating.

Exercises to Explore at Home

The Mirror Exercise

Although somatic work is best done with a therapist, I want to offer a few exercises that can be done at home. These exercises should complement your therapy, and you may continue using them throughout your life as needed, even after extensive trauma work. I consider these exercises somatic regulatory practices, and we will always need access to somatic regulation.

One such exercise is the mirror exercise. In this practice, I invite clients to set a timer for three minutes, find a mirror, and look into their own eyes. I often joke that initially you'll find yourself noticing your hair, your eyebrows, your pores—all kinds of things—but eventually, you'll focus on your eyes. Connect with your eyes and your breath. See if you can sense or feel the person you are looking at. Ask yourself who this person is and what emotions arise when you look at them. Look for your inner child in the reflection. Recognize that this is the only person on the planet who knows every part of your story.

Can you truly see yourself?
Do you know who this is?
What emotions come up for you?
When was the last time you really saw yourself?

Take time to journal about this experience, and share your reflections with your therapist for further processing. There is no right or wrong way to feel during this. Even if you can't complete the exercise, that is important! You can not fail here.

The next time you try this exercise, increase the time to four minutes. Continue gradually increasing the duration until you can connect with yourself for about ten minutes without feeling the urge to look away. I still do this exercise myself. When I'm feeling frazzled, disconnected, or lost, I make time for it. We often get so caught up in the external world that we lose touch with ourselves. We forget that we, too, are human beings who deserve our own attention. I encourage clients to try this exercise even in the middle of an argument with a friend or partner. Afterward, return to the practice, reconnect with yourself, and then return to the conversation.

The Bioenergetic Bendover

Grounding is a crucial regulation skill. Many of us are familiar with grounding techniques like identifying five blue things in a room to anchor our minds. Somatic grounding, however, focuses on getting into your body and feeling safe there. One effective bioenergetic grounding technique is to start by placing your feet hip-width apart, slightly bending your knees, so they are not locked. Close your eyes and take a deep breath in through your nose and out through your mouth. Feel your breath move all the way from your pelvic floor to your chest. Take about three deep, slow breaths in this way. Some people find it helpful to place one hand on their chest and the other on their stomach during this part.

After three to five breaths, bend your knees slightly, and allow the upper half of your body to fold forward until your hands can touch the ground. Continue breathing in through your nose and out through your mouth, while consciously asking the upper half of your body (arms, hands, neck, face, shoulders, chest, upper and lower back) to release any tension. Only your legs should hold tension—make sure your knees remain unlocked and slightly bent. Stay in this position for around three to five minutes. With each exhale, focus on releasing more tension from the upper half of your body. Feel free to make sounds as you exhale. Notice if you struggle while doing this. Are you feeling rushed? Do you feel the urge to do something else? How does it feel to make noise with your exhale? Reflect on how you feel before and after the exercise.

Connection Exercise

It's important to have someone you trust deeply for this exercise. This can be a friend, family member, partner, or therapist—someone with whom you feel safe connecting, even if you don't always feel that way. Before starting, share with them that you'd like to do a connection exercise that may be intense for both of you. Let them know they can stop the exercise at any time if it becomes too overwhelming, and that you can do the same. Set a timer for five minutes. Sit across from the person you've chosen and make eye contact. Breathe deeply. There should be no talking—just eye contact and breathing.

If you begin to feel unsafe, you can stop the exercise, ask for reassurance, or simply close your eyes and return to the connection when you're ready. How does it feel to sit in raw connection with someone? What thoughts arise as you settle into the connection? What sensations are present in your body? Journal about your experience and share it with your therapist.

Other Somatic Methods to Consider

Because I have found bioenergetic analysis to be useful in my work, I focused this book on it to describe the armoring patterns related to childhood trauma and the coinciding treatments using this method. This is a modality I don't see talked about enough, and I wanted to shift that. Bioenergetic Analysis specifically addresses discharging trauma from the body, reducing chronic tension and emotional repression to help individuals feel more grounded in their body.

However, several other modalities are helpful, most of which I utilize in some way in my work. Somatic therapies such as psychodrama, breathwork, Eye Movement Desensitization and Reprocessing (EMDR), Internal Family Systems (IFS), and others are my primary recommendations for individuals seeking deep-level healing. Personally, when I work with any other somatic modalities that I am trained in, I still utilize my knowledge of the armoring patterns to help navigate any blind spots in the therapy. I look for the armoring patterns to help formulate a plan to approach the client's concerns. In my work, I often integrate bioenergetics, EMDR, psychodrama, breathwork, and an IFS-informed framework, depending on what presents.

If you have gone through individual, couples, or family therapy and have benefited, but still feel your trauma is armoring you, somatic therapy is the next step. Traditional talk therapy can also be a somatic therapy if the body is brought into it. Therapies such as Cognitive Behavioral Therapy (CBT), Dialectical Behavior Therapy (DBT), Client-Centered Therapy, psychoanalysis, and other primarily cognitive talk therapies are helpful and provide benefits. Everyone should consider this sort of therapy, whether or not they ultimately end up in my office. I think it can significantly reduce symptoms of mental health struggles, and for some, this is enough. However, talk therapy, which generally addresses beliefs, ideas, conscious feelings, and theories, will only get us so far.

We are more than our brains; we are our bodies. Therefore, we need to bring both into the therapeutic relationship for long-term and sustainable healing to occur. Some individuals recognize the pain and aches in their body that don't go away. Or they notice that sorting through challenging thoughts and emotions is too complicated. Maybe they can't stop flipping into "rage mode," no matter how hard they try to challenge those thoughts. They recognize the lack of intrinsic peace in their minds and bodies. These are the people who end up in my office needing something that other therapies don't offer—somatic healing.

Treatment modalities such as Dialectical Behavioral Therapy, Cognitive Behavioral Therapy, Person-Centered talk therapy, and more are highly beneficial. Somatic treatments are most helpful for those who have done traditional talk therapies and require additional healing. I believe all therapy should have a somatic component to address the multifaceted trauma impact. This can include massages, acupuncture, ortho-bionomy, or physical fitness, such as yoga. However, I also acknowledge that I don't know everything, and some individuals find tremendous relief and healing in talk therapies alone.

Bioenergetic Therapy: Integrating the Body and Mind

Bioenergetic Analysis, developed by Alexander Lowen in the 1950s, is a body-oriented psychotherapy that emphasizes the connection between emotional well-being and physical vitality. The therapy operates under the premise that the body stores trauma, repressed emotions, and unexpressed psychological conflicts, which can manifest as chronic muscle tension, posture distortions, and energy blockages. Bioenergetic therapy uses physical exercises, breathing techniques, and verbal expression to release physical tensions and promote a healthier flow of energy, which leads to emotional release and greater psychological integration.

Bioenergetic therapy targets "character structures" (what I labeled armoring patterns) that individuals develop in response to early emotional pain. By focusing on bodily sensations and encouraging clients to engage with their physical experiences, Bioenergetic therapy breaks down the barriers to emotional expression and fosters self-awareness. The therapeutic process often includes exercises designed to bring attention to breathing, grounding, and bodily sensations, enabling individuals to access and process deep-seated emotional material.

The body-oriented nature of Bioenergetic Therapy has generated interest among researchers seeking to explore the mind-body connection in therapeutic contexts. Many studies have demonstrated that Bioenergetic exercises significantly reduced symptoms of anxiety and depression in participants. Bourguignon's study explored the efficacy of Bioenergetic Analysis in treating mental health conditions like depression and anxiety.[28] The research found that combining Bioenergetic therapy with traditional talk therapy led to significant improvements in emotional regulation, as well as a reduction in somatic symptoms related to depression. Participants reported feeling more grounded and relaxed, highlighting the therapeutic potential of Bioenergetic techniques in addressing both psychological and physical aspects of mental health and the importance of integrating body-focused therapies into mental health treatment plans for holistic healing.

Though fewer large-scale studies have been conducted compared to other therapeutic modalities like EMDR, the available evidence supports Bioenergetic therapy as an effective tool for addressing somatic complaints, chronic tension, and emotional trauma. It is important to note that Bioenergetic therapy may not be suitable for all clients, particularly those who have significant physical limitations or difficulties engaging in physical exercises. Due to the intense nature of Bioenergetic Analysis, I always recommend that a client complete some talk therapy before participating in it.

EMDR Therapy: Reprocessing Trauma Through Bilateral Stimulation

In the late 1980s, Francine Shapiro developed EMDR as a therapeutic approach for individuals with post-traumatic stress disorder. The core mechanism behind EMDR involves reprocessing distressing memories by using bilateral stimulation, typically through guided eye movements. This process is believed to activate both hemispheres of the brain, helping the brain to process and integrate traumatic memories in a healthier way, reducing their emotional charge and intrusive nature. EMDR is based on the Adaptive Information

Processing (AIP) model, which posits that trauma disrupts normal memory processing, leading to maladaptive memories that are not fully integrated into the individual's larger life narrative. The bilateral stimulation in EMDR is thought to facilitate the brain's natural ability to process and resolve traumatic material, allowing the individual to reframe distressing memories in a less emotionally charged context.

Numerous studies have supported the efficacy of EMDR, particularly in the treatment of PTSD. Additionally, van der Kolk, a leading figure in trauma research, highlighted EMDR's effectiveness in helping individuals with chronic PTSD and dissociative symptoms.[29] The therapy has also shown promise in addressing complex trauma, as evidenced by studies that found significant improvements in patients with CPTSD following EMDR treatment.[30] It is important to note that there is ongoing debate about the specific role of bilateral stimulation in the efficacy of EMDR. Despite these limitations, EMDR remains a popular and well-regarded option for trauma therapy. I have used EMDR in my practice and witnessed healing for many individuals.

Psychodrama Therapy

Psychodrama, developed by Jacob and Zerka Moreno in the 1920s, uses dramatic techniques and role-playing to help individuals explore and reframe personal experiences. In a typical psychodrama session, the client (referred to as the "protagonist") is encouraged to enact scenes from their life, past, or future, often using other group members as auxiliary egos to play significant roles. The therapist guides the process, encouraging exploration of underlying emotions and the resolution of conflicts through dramatic action.

Psychodrama is grounded in the belief that enactment allows individuals to gain insight into their psychological conflicts and release pent-up emotions. The therapeutic setting provides a safe space for the protagonist to explore difficult situations from a new perspective, which can lead to cognitive reframing and emotional release. Techniques such as "role reversal," in which the client takes on the role of another person involved in a conflict, allow for a deeper understanding of interpersonal dynamics.

The therapeutic impact of Psychodrama has been widely studied in group therapy settings. Blatner's meta-analysis revealed that psychodramatic techniques were particularly effective in treating individuals with interpersonal difficulties, depression, and anxiety.[31] One randomized controlled trial by Kipper found that psychodrama significantly reduced symptoms of depression and anxiety compared to a wait-list control group.[32]

The group nature of Psychodrama is a crucial factor in its effectiveness. It brings together somatic work and connection, which can be a barrier to treatment as discussed in the previous chapter. Furthermore, its ability to tap into unconscious material through action rather than verbal communication can facilitate breakthroughs in clients who have difficulty expressing themselves in traditional therapeutic settings.

Psychodrama may be more beneficial for individuals who enjoy or are open to engaging in dramatic, action-based methods of self-exploration. The process can be emotionally intense, and some individuals may find it overwhelming, especially those with more fragile emotional states or a history of severe trauma. Additionally, while research on Psychodrama is promising, we need more studies with rigorous methodological designs to further substantiate its efficacy across different populations. Psychodrama integrates beautifully with bioenergetics, and many bioenergetic practitioners utilize this as part of their work with their clients.

Internal Family Systems: Treatment of Our Parts

Dr. Richard Schwartz developed Internal Family Systems (IFS) in the 1980s. IFS is based on the idea that the mind is made up of multiple subpersonalities, or "parts," each with its own beliefs, desires, and emotions. These parts can be seen as different aspects of the self, often in conflict with one another, contributing to emotional pain and psychological distress. This therapy is extremely beneficial on its own or integrated with other approaches such as EMDR or bioenergetics. It helps us understand that we can have one part of us that hates our parents and another that deeply loves our parents. It helps to separate how we feel from who we are, which is extremely important when we're trying to navigate around ego defenses.

IFS suggests that each person has a core self that is inherently wise, compassionate, and capable of healing. IFS therapy helps individuals identify and understand their internal parts, and through dialogue and integration, restore balance and harmony within the system of the mind. This model has gained traction not only as a psychological treatment but also as a somatic intervention, as it incorporates awareness of bodily sensations that are often linked to unresolved emotions and trauma.

The mechanism of action in IFS is rooted in the therapeutic relationship, the exploration of parts, and the cultivation of the self. The therapist helps clients recognize and differentiate between their various internal parts, including those that are protective (e.g., the manager or firefighters) and those that may have been wounded in past experiences (e.g., the exile). By encouraging clients to approach these parts with compassion and curiosity, IFS aims to reduce the internal conflict and trauma that often manifest as mental health disorders such as depression, anxiety, or PTSD. IFS also emphasizes the importance of somatic awareness, with clients guided to notice physical sensations that may signal the activation of different parts. Integrating these parts, guided by the Self, can lead to profound psychological healing.

Research on the efficacy of IFS has shown promising results. One study found a clinically significant reduction in post-traumatic stress symptoms when IFS was utilized.[33] Furthermore, recent clinical trials have supported using IFS to treat depression, anxiety, and borderline personality disorder, demonstrating that patients experienced significant symptom reduction and improved functioning. A meta-analysis by Schlapfer concluded that IFS was particularly effective for individuals with complex trauma, as the approach's focus on integration and healing of fragmented parts helped create a sense of internal coherence and stability.[34] These findings suggest that IFS can be a powerful and effective therapeutic approach, especially when traditional methods fall short.

Breathwork

Through my study of Bioenergetic Analysis, I have learned that breath is one of the most healing functions of our body. I received training specifically in breathwork in order to integrate more knowledge of the healing power of our breath into my work. I combine breathwork and Bioenergetic Analysis for some of the most intense and incredible healing work

In my work, breathing brings out emotion, not minimizes or suppresses it. Imagine a little child trying to stop crying; they hold their breath because they intuitively know that if they don't breathe, they don't feel. Much of the breathwork I encourage my clients to do enhances deep breathing to bring out emotions deeply locked in the body.

Bioenergetic Analysis includes breathwork exercises in the modality. However, many specific breathwork processes, some of which I have utilized and experienced, have huge implications for treating trauma and other mental health and physical illnesses. Breathwork, a practice that involves consciously controlling the breath, has emerged as an effective therapeutic tool for addressing trauma. Trauma can significantly disrupt the autonomic nervous system, leading to symptoms such as hyperarousal, dissociation, and chronic stress. Breathwork helps to regulate this system, promoting relaxation, emotional regulation, and physical healing.

There are many forms of breathwork that allow different methods of healing. I tend to focus on breathwork that activates the release of emotions, not calms them. One method that allows activation of the nervous system for emotional release is Holotropic Breathwork. This therapeutic technique was developed in the 1960s by Czech psychiatrist Dr. Stanislav Grof and his wife, Christina Grof, as a non-pharmacological alternative to psychedelic therapy.[35] The method combines accelerated breathing, evocative music, and focused bodywork to induce non-ordinary states of consciousness, facilitating deep self-exploration and emotional healing. Drawing inspiration from ancient practices like Pranayama and modern transpersonal psychology, Holotropic Breathwork aims to help individuals access unconscious material, release repressed emotions, and achieve a sense of integration and wholeness. It has been utilized in various therapeutic and personal growth settings, offering participants profound experiences of emotional release, catharsis, and spiritual insight. The development of this technique has led to many different forms of similar breathing techniques designed to allow for deep emotional release.

Many researchers have taken an interest in breathwork modalities due to the recent investigation into psychedelic-assisted therapies and their use in treating trauma. Eyerman (2013) conducted a 12-year clinical report examining the use of Holotropic Breathwork (HB) in a community hospital setting with over 11,000 psychiatric inpatients.[36] The weekly, group-based HB sessions were offered to patients who had no prior spiritual or HB experience and came from a range of specialized units, including those for sexual trauma, dual diagnosis, substance dependence, mood disorders, adolescents, and acute psychosis. Over the entire study period, neither patients nor staff reported any adverse reactions.

Researchers did not track individual diagnoses and treatment outcomes but did collect qualitative data from 482 participants. Their self-reported experiences reflected the four categories outlined by the Grofs: physical-sensory, biographical, perinatal, and transpersonal, with 82 percent of participants reporting a transpersonal experience during at least one session. Many patients described HB as the most impactful therapy they received during their hospital stay.

Eyerman concluded that Holotropic Breathwork appears to be a low-risk, potentially beneficial therapeutic practice for addressing a wide variety of psychological and existential challenges. I have seen breathwork modalities provide deep and profound healing to my clients, which mirrors other anecdotal reports, much like this study. However, more research is needed.

The breath can help trauma survivors in many ways during their healing journey. Some breathing techniques activate the nervous system and release pent-up emotion, such as those mentioned above. Other methods allow for the calming and regulation of the nervous system. Our breath truly contains everything we need for our healing journey. A study found that controlled breathing techniques significantly reduced PTSD symptoms, including hyperarousal and intrusive thoughts, by modulating the autonomic nervous system.[37] Overall, various forms of breathwork offer a valuable, accessible method for trauma healing, addressing both the psychological and physiological aspects of trauma.

Its use as part of a comprehensive trauma treatment plan is supported by growing evidence of its positive impact on trauma recovery. I have seen breathwork provide deep healing to my clients during our sessions.

CHAPTER 11

ALLIES IN HEALING

> *Therapy takes us backward into a forgotten past,
> but this was not a safe and secure time, else we would not
> have emerged from it scarred by battle wounds
> and armoured in self-defense.*
> —Dr. Alexander Lowen

The truth is, a therapist and a client are partners in the healing journey. Neither has all the answers. Healing will be a collaborative process that allows the client's truth, expressed through their emotions and the intuition of their body, that will allow the healing to occur. The client and therapist must be a good fit in working together for this to take place. The client's desire to heal must be larger than the fear to heal, and the therapist's ego must take a back seat to the client's intuition.

I am not claiming to be an exceptional healer or all-knowing expert. I am a human who, honestly, finds it much easier to recount all this information in a calm and cozy book-writing session than in a therapy session. However, I have been a healer to some and have been grounded enough to help them release the struggles I laid out in this book. During some sessions, I missed things, and then caught them with enough time to continue our work. Sometimes, I have missed other things and allowed my countertransference to take over and reenact patterns, creating a dynamic of resentment from the client or myself that caused the therapy to terminate before the client got what they needed. I am human and not perfect, and recognizing this within myself allows me to do the deep work my clients deserve. I show up as a human, connected with the wisdom of my body and the knowledge of my conscious mind. I come prepared to honor the connection with my client and follow their body's wisdom.

Therapy can be a messy process for the therapist and the client. This level of deep healing is often chaotic, and the relationship between the client and therapist is of the utmost importance. It is crucial for the client to share the transference, any feelings they have towards the therapist, because that is their body's wisdom. The therapist needs to be in their body and become close friends with their countertransference, feelings they are having towards the client, because that is their body's wisdom. In some counseling models, therapists are taught to know their countertransference; however, they understand it is their work, not the client's. My greatest bioenergetic teachers taught me that this is not always true.

It is important to feel into your countertransference and know whether it is you, the therapist, the client, or both of you triggering a response. In my experience, nearly one hundred percent of the time, it is both. The transference in the client triggers countertransference in the therapist's body and vice versa, much like other relationships. Our bodies do not care about the role we take on in our heads as "the therapist" or "the client." Our body still does what it is taught to do—respond to stimuli, underlying energy, and cues. The idea that the client should not emotionally impact their therapist and a therapist should not emotionally impact their client only creates a larger divide for the therapist and their relationship with their body. This divide leads therapists to experience burnout, resent the work, and become rigid and guarded. It is important to use countertransference and transference as information, not inspiration for action.

Therapists must have healthy boundaries, so they don't need to disconnect from their bodies to protect themselves from clients. They need to know themselves well enough to know how to be in themselves and with the client; the only appropriate way to be with a client is to be with themselves, much like any other relationship. I am deeply connected to my clients. I think of them often and feel their pain as I sit in it. I am not afraid.

From Soldier to Civilian

Comparing trauma to war seemed drastic when I first thought about it. However, with time and experience, working with individuals who face trauma, I think it is an accurate representation. This does not minimize the military members who go to war to fight for our freedom. However, individuals in our society are fighting daily for their own individual freedom and sometimes even their lives. Some make it, some stay in the battle forever, and others die from it. Individuals die daily due to physical and emotional repercussions of trauma, from deaths by suicide to physical disease. Fully recognizing the war we are in and the consequences we face is, I hope, the first step of ending this lifelong battle.

My goal in writing this book is to help trauma survivors lay down the armor they had to wear in response to their trauma and instead don armor that serves them in their lives. I hope to inspire and validate mental health practitioners to approach healing with their clients using a deep lens based in humanity and understanding that their clients know how to heal; they only need to be taught how to allow themselves to follow their body's lead. I aim to inspire providers to continuously learn more about the body and mind's natural mechanisms from healing and the neurobiology that validates somatic healing. Also, I want to encourage those who are living as trauma soldiers to lay down their armor and learn to live, as scary as that may be. I hope to inspire them to, in healthy ways, challenge systems, familial and otherwise, that oppress them. I hope to invite trauma survivors to choose healing and choose themselves.

One of my aspirations for writing this book is to spread the word: healing is possible and is, evolutionarily, what your brain and body are designed to do. The idea that you are broken due to your trauma and, therefore, cannot recover is defeating and false. Healing is possible; you can have hope. Your brain and body may have adapted to the trauma, but they can adapt to living again under the right circumstances and with the right environment for healing. Through healing, your body and mind can begin to recognize that the war has ended and you are safe. When the ceasefire occurs, you can come home to yourself and your body. You can feel, breathe, and move through life as if your life is for you. You can possess the one thing you have in this life from birth to death—yourself.

Healing is possible; you can have hope.

ENDNOTES

1. Bourguignon, C., Piot, J., and Gauthier, L. (2016). Efficacy of Bioenergetic Analysis in the Treatment of Depression and Anxiety. *Journal of Body-Oriented Psychotherapy*, 15, no. 2 (2016): 87-102.
2. Beck, Aaron T. *Depression: Clinical, Experimental and Theoretical Aspects.* New York: Harper and Row, 1967.
3. Van der Kolk, Bessel. A. *The body keeps the score: Brain, mind, and body in the healing of trauma.* New York: Viking, 2014.
4. Felitti, V.J., R. F. Anda, D. Nordenberg, D.F. Williamson, A. M. Spitz, V. Edwards, M. P. Koss, and J. S. Marks. "Relationship of Childhood Abuse and Household Dysfunction to Many of the Leading Causes of Death in Adults. The Adverse Childhood Experiences (ACE) Study. *American Journal of Preventive Medicine*, 14, no. 4 (1998): 245-58. DOI: 10.1016/s0749-3797(98)00017-8.
5. Inyang, Bithaiah, Faisal J. Gondal, Godwin A. Abah, Mahesh Minnal Dhandapani, Manasa Manne, Manish Khanna, Sabitha Challa, et al. "The Role of Childhood Trauma in Psychosis and Schizophrenia: A Systematic Review." *Cureus*, 14, no. 1 (2022): e21466. DOI: 10.7759/cureus.21466.
6. Lang, Adelheid, Peter Ott, Renata del Giudice, and Manuel Schabus. "Memory Traces Formed in Utero—Newborns' Autonomic and Neuronal Responses to Prenatal Stimuli and the Maternal Voice." *Brain Sciences*, 10, no. 11 (2020): 837. https://doi.org/10.3390/brainsci10110837.

7   Yehuda, Rachel and Amy Lehrner. "Intergenerational Transmission of Trauma Effects: Putative Role of Epigenetic Mechanisms." *World Psychiatry* 17, no. 3 (2018): 243-257. DOI: 10.1002/wps.20568.

8   Levine, Peter A. *Trauma and memory: Brain and Body in a Search for the Living Past.* New York: The Guilford Press, 2015.

9   Lowen, Alexander. *Bioenergetics: The Revolutionary Therapy That Uses the Language of the Body to Heal the Problems of the Mind.* New York: Penguin Books, 1976.

10 Heim, C., D. J. Newport, S. Heit, Y. P. Graham, M. Wilcox, R. Bonsall, A. H. Miller, et al. "Pituitary-Adrenal and Autonomic Responses to Stress in Women after Sexual and Physical Abuse in Childhood." *Journal of the American Medical Association,* 284, no. 5 (2000): 592-7. DOI: 10.1001/jama.284.5.592.

11 Kendall-Tackett, Kathleen. "Psychological Trauma and Physical Health: A Psychoneuroimmunology Approach to Etiology of Negative Health Effects and Possible Interventions." *Psychological Trauma: Theory, Research, Practice, and Policy,* 1 no. 1 (2009): 35–48. https://doi.org/10.1037/a0015128.

12 Felitti, V. J.

13 Bower, Gordon H., and Heidi Sivers. "Cognitive Impact of Traumatic Events." *Development and Psychopathology,* 10, no. 4 (1998): 625–53. https://doi.org/10.1017/s0954579498001795.

14 Lowen, A. (1971). *The language of the body.* Collier Books.

15 Van der Kolk, Bessel A..

16 Perry, B. D. "The neuroarcheology of childhood maltreatment: The neurodevelopmental costs of adverse childhood events." In *The cost of child maltreatment: Who*

pays? Robert A. Geffner and Robert Falconer (eds.) San Diego: Family Violence and Sexual Assault Institute, 2001.

17   Siegel, Daniel J. *The Developing Mind: How Relationships and the Brain Interact to Shape Who We Are* (2nd ed.). New York: The Guilford Press, 2012.

18   Brown, Vanessa M. and Rajendra A. Morey. "Neural Systems for Cognitive and Emotional Processing in Posttraumatic Stress Disorder." *Frontiers in Psychology*, 3 (2012): 449. DOI: 10.3389/fpsyg.2012.00449.

19   UCSF Center to Advance Trauma Informed Care. "How Trauma Affects Our Health." University of California San Francisco. Accessed April 28, 2025. https://cthc.ucsf.edu/why-trauma/#:~:text=Key%20Research%20Findings%20About%20Adverse,more%20likely%20to%20smoke%20cigarettes.

20   UCSF Center to Advance Trauma Informed Care.

21   Hughes, Virginia. "The Orphanage Problem. *National Geographic*. July 31, 2013. https://www.nationalgeographic.com/science/article/the-orphanage-problem.

22   Holt-Lunstad, Julieanne. "Social Connection as a Critical Factor for Mental and Physical Health: Evidence, Trends, Challenges, and Future Implications." *World Psychiatry*, 23, no. 3 (2024): 312-32. https://doi.org/10.1002/wps.21224.

23   Martino, Jessica, Jennifer Pegg, and Elizabeth Pegg Frates. "The Connection Prescription: Using the Power of Social Interactions and the Deep Desire for Connectedness to Empower Health and Wellness." *American Journal of Lifestyle Medicine*, 11, no. 6 (2015): 466-75. DOI: 10.1177/1559827615608788.

24   Gage, Suzanne H. and Harry R. Sumnall. (2019). "Rat Park: How a Rat Paradise Changed the Narrative of Addiction." *Addiction*, 114, no. 5 (2019): 917–22. https://doi.org/10.1111/add.14481.

25 Brown, Brené. (2012). *Daring Greatly: How the Courage to Be Vulnerable Transforms the Way We Live, Love, Parent, and Lead.* New York: Gotham Books, 2012.

26 Crenshaw, Kimberle. "Mapping the Margins: Intersectionality, Identity Politics, and Violence against Women of Color." *Stanford Law Review*, 43, no. 6 (1991): 1241-99. https://doi.org/10.2307/1229039.

27 Firth, Joseph, James E. Gangwisch, Alessandra Borsini, Robyn E. Wootton, and Emeran A. Mayer. "Food and Mood: How Do Diet and Nutrition Affect Mental Wellbeing?" *British Medical Journal*, 369 (2020): m2382. DOI: 10.1136/bmj.m2382.

28 Bourguignon, C., J. Piot, and L. Gauthier. (2016).

29 Van der Kolk, Bessel. A. *The body keeps the score: Brain, mind, and body in the healing of trauma.* New York: Viking, 2014.

30 Melegkovits, Eirini, Jocelyn Blumberg, Emily Dixon, Kimberley Ehntholt, Julia Gillard, Hamodi Kayal, Tim Kember, et al. "The Effectiveness of Trauma-Focused Psychotherapy for Complex Post-Traumatic Stress Disorder: A Retrospective Study. *European Psychiatry*, 66, no. 1 (2022): e4. doi: 10.1192/j.eurpsy.2022.2346.

31 Blatner, Adam. *Psychodrama: Role Playing in Social Work and Therapy*. Fourth ed. Springer Publishing Company, 2000. https://psycnet.apa.org/record/2000-07509-000

32 Kipper, D. A. and T. D. Ritchie. "The Effectiveness of Psychodramatic Techniques: A Meta-Analysis. 2003. In: Database of Abstracts of Reviews of Effects (DARE): Quality-Assessed Reviews [Internet]. York (UK): Centre for Reviews and Dissemination (UK); 1995-. Available from: https://www.ncbi.nlm.nih.gov/books/NBK69723/.

33 Hodgdon, Hilary B., Frank G. Anderson, Elizabeth Southwell, Wendy Hrubec, and Richard Schwartz. (2021). "Internal Family Systems (IFS) Therapy for Posttraumatic

Stress Disorder (PTSD) among Survivors of Multiple Childhood Trauma: A Pilot Effectiveness Study." *Journal of Aggression, Maltreatment & Trauma*, 31, no. 1 (2021): 22–43. https://doi.org/10.1080/10926771.2021.2013375.

34 Schlapfer, T. E., et al. "Meta-Analysis of the Efficacy of Internal Family Systems Therapy: Impact on Psychological and Somatic Symptoms." *International Journal of Psychotherapy*, 21, no. 2 (2017): 139-50.

35 Holotropic Sydney. (n.d.). *What is the history of Holotropic Breathwork*. Retrieved May 9, 2025, from https://holotropicsydney.com.au/resources/what-is-the-history-of-holotropic-breathwork

36 Eyerman, James. (2013). A Clinical Report of Holotropic Breathwork in 11,000 Psychiatric Inpatients in a Community Hospital Setting. *MAPS Bulletin*, 23, no. 1, (2013): 24–7. https://maps.org/news-letters/v23n1/v23n1_p24-27.pdf.

37 Kim, Sang Hwan, Suzanne M. Schneider, Margaret Bevans, Len Kravitz, Christine Mermier, Clifford Qualls, and Mark R. Burge. "PTSD Symptom Reduction With Mindfulness-Based Stretching and Deep Breathing Exercise: Randomized Controlled Clinical Trial of Efficacy." *The Journal of Clinical Endocrinology & Metabolism*, 98, no. 7 (2013): 2984–92. https://doi.org/10.1210/jc.2012-3742.

ACKNOWLEDGMENTS

To my mother, Theresa. I began writing this book immediately following her death because I felt her armour as I hugged her for the last time. Mom, you were never fully free but always encouraged me to be. Thank you.

To my father, Richard, who never got a chance to fully live. Your death was part of the trauma that built me, and also, your love was part of the energy that healed me. I miss you. Thank you.

To my Armenian grandparents, George and Clara, whose parents and relatives survived genocide. Even through all this, you encouraged and provided a base for us to find a meaningful life. Thank you.

To my Nana, Doris Rose, whose eyes twitched from abuse, but no one said anything. She slept with her shoes on to be ready if she needed to jump up. She fought for me but never for herself. Nana, thank you for helping to shape me into the person I am today through your wisdom.

I also dedicate this book to my husband, Brian, who exudes kindness and has taught me that I no longer have to be a soldier. Other relationships reinforced my armor. Your gentleness and compassion inspired me to work to continue to put it down. My soul loves you. I see you sincerely and genuinely, and I know you see me. I love you the most—I win.

To my sisters, Jamie and Kristin. You two fight battles every day, just like I have, to put down your armor. We are the generation that speaks out, cries out, and screams at the top of our lungs that this is the generation that stops this cycle. We are the soldiers who will end the war, the powerful three.

I couldn't fight without your understanding, your mistakes, and your love. "Your blood, my blood, our blood."—*Practical Magic*

To my children who inspire me daily to further learn about myself and my armor. I will always work to be the best version of myself, so that you can be the best versions of yourselves, carrying as little armor as possible. I promise to do my best not to wear my armor, so you won't have to wear yours.

To my niece and nephew, thank you for reminding me what joy and connection look like. Thank you for being a part of my heart. Keep smiling and expressing everything you think and feel! You inspire me.

To my best friend since childhood, Jessica. You chose to walk that journey with us. You are such a huge part of why I am who I am. When we were kids, you made yourself uncomfortable by trying to help me when I needed help, even if I didn't want it at the time. Thank you.

To my brothers-in-law, Trevon and Patrick. Thank you for choosing to be a part of our battles. Thank you for loving us through our battles while fighting battles of your own. You may not always understand what you signed up for, but you work to understand, and for this, I am beyond grateful.

To my living relatives, you are the survivors. You have taught my sisters and me how to survive, even if you didn't always know how. Thank you.

To my in-laws, Steve and Brenda, who help care for my little ones while I learn, grow, and work. Thank you for loving my boys so much that I have the space to do the work I love, to be better for them, and create a better life for them. Thank you for the amazing son you helped to shape.

To all my friends and family, I may not have been individually mentioned here, you know who you are. Thank you for being a part of my life and my story. Thank you for sharing with me your struggles and triumphs around a fire, at a table, or in passing. Thank you for helping me put down floors, paint offices, peel wallpaper, and anything else I've ever needed. Thank you for always showing up to fight alongside me in whatever battle life brings.

Dr. Elias, my Armenian ally and friend. From teaching me how to navigate my way around town to giving me a start in private practice to teaching me much of what I know. I can not thank you enough for your guidance, love, and support.

Randy, you told me I should go to a workshop at the Florida School for Bioenergetic Analysis when I was a young graduate student. You changed my life by gently pushing me to do that. Not just my professional life, but my personal life as well. Thank you.

Dr. Bob and Susan, you both changed my life with the school you created. The Florida School for Bioenergetic Analysis has changed countless lives internationally; mine was no exception. I carry on the work I learned from you. Thank you.

Tom, you have been my greatest ally in this bioenergetic work, whether you realize it or not. You have taught me so much through humor and tears. Thank you.

Eric. Thank you for being my first bioenergetic therapist and so much more. Thank you for your wisdom, your jokes, your music, and being an important part of many steps in my life.

All of my peers in the Florida Society for Bioenergetic Analysis, you all taught me so much. The years I spent watching you all stand bravely on the farmhouse floor and scream, cry, laugh, and dance were truly the most developmental years of my life. I grew up in that farmhouse and you were my parents, siblings, friends, and ancestors. You know who you are. Thank you.

To all of my colleagues at Gainesville Healing House, thank you for growing with me every single day, week, and month. Thank you for teaching me and hearing me. Thank you for rooting for those you hear screaming from my office. I truly love each of you.

To my clients. You may consider yourselves my students, but you are equally my teachers. Every one of you is special to me. I see you. I am with you, always. Thank you for your trust and bravery; thank you for the honor of being a healing witness in your journey. I can not express how humbled and honored I feel.

ABOUT THE AUTHOR

Kelly Nenezian is a psychotherapist, trainer, and business owner from Florida. She holds a B.S. in Microbiology and Cell Science from the University of Florida and a Master of Science in Counseling Psychology from Nova Southeastern University. After graduating, she completed her post-graduate internship in a residential facility where she treated individuals suffering from mental health conditions and addictions.

Consequently, she began her extensive healing and learning journey of Bioenergetic Analysis through the Florida Society of Bioenergetic Analysis (FSBA) to help clients access deeper levels of healing through somatic work. After experiencing her own deep-level healing, she started her first Bioenergetic group in the residential facility. Clients genuinely changed as they did the difficult somatic work in the group. Since then, Kelly has helped adolescents, adults, couples, families, and seniors manage and recover from trauma, depression, anxiety, and other disorders. She practiced individual and group therapy methods to promote healing. In addition, Kelly is an EMDR Certified Therapist and FSBA Certified Bioenergetic Therapist. She also gained experience helping individuals learn to manage disorders such as ADHD, OCD, personality disorders, and more.

Kelly opened her practice, Gainesville Healing House, in 2017 to provide deep-level healing through many modalities, especially somatic-informed interventions. In 2020, she founded the not-for-profit Healing For All, Inc., providing access to mental health services for underserved populations. Kelly is also actively involved in the Florida Society of Bioenergetic Analysis, where she is now a trainer and director.

CONNECT WITH KELLY

Follow her on your favorite social media platforms today.

@KellyNenezian

GainesvilleHealingHouse.com

LEARN MORE ABOUT GAINESVILLE HEALING HOUSE

Helping You Light Your Path

Follow them on your favorite social media platforms today.

@GainesvilleHealingHouse

GainesvilleHealingHouse.com

RECONNECT. RELEASE. RECLAIM.

Reclaim Your Life with Somatic Therapy

Are you carrying stress, trauma, or emotional tension that no amount of talking seems to fix? Your body holds the key to deep, lasting healing—and somatic therapy can help you unlock it.

Somatic Therapy is a gentle, body-based approach to healing that goes beyond the mind. Through guided movement, breathwork, and embodied awareness, you'll learn to release trauma stored in the nervous system, restore balance, and reclaim your sense of safety, joy, and vitality.

GainesvilleHealingHouse.com

THIS BOOK IS PROTECTED INTELLECTUAL PROPERTY

The author of this book values Intellectual Property. The book you just read is protected by Instant IP[IP], a proprietary process, which integrates blockchain technology giving Intellectual Property "Global Protection." By creating a "Time-Stamped" smart contract that can never be tampered with or changed, we establish "First Use" that tracks back to the author.

Instant IP[IP] functions much like a Pre-Patent since it provides an immutable "First Use" of the Intellectual Property. This is achieved through our proprietary process of leveraging blockchain technology and smart contracts. As a result, proving "First Use" is simple through a global and verifiable smart contract. By protecting intellectual property with blockchain technology and smart contracts, we establish a "First to File" event.

Protected by Instant IP[IP]

LEARN MORE AT INSTANTIP.TODAY

www.ingramcontent.com/pod-product-compliance
Lightning Source LLC
Chambersburg PA
CBHW031151020426
42333CB00013B/618